DIVING AND SNORKELING

S The eychelles

Lawson Wood

Pisces Books®

**Pisces Books**®

Copyright © 1996 by Lonely Planet Publications
Head Office: PO Box 617, Hawthorn, Vic 3122, Australia
Branches: 155 Filbert St, Suite 251, Oakland, CA 94607, USA
                    10a Spring Place, London NW5 3BH, UK
                    71 bis rue du Cardinal Lemoine, 75005 Paris, France

Printed in Hong Kong

Library of Congress Cataloging-in-Publication Data

Wood, Lawson
       Diving and snorkeling guide to The Seychelles / Lawson Wood.
       p.   cm.
       Includes bibliographical references and index.
       ISBN 1-55992-097-1
       1. Deep diving—Seychelles—Guidebooks.   2. Snorkeling—
Seychelles—Guidebooks.   3. Seychelles—Guidebooks.   I. Title.
II. Title: Seychelles.
GV840.S78W66   1997
797.2′3′09696—dc20   96-42214
                                                                                    CIP

PHOTOGRAPHY

The author's photographs were taken using Nikonos 111, Nikonos
1VA, Nikonos V, Nikon F-801, Nikon F-90, and the Pentax LX. Lenses used on the amphibious Nikonos system were 35mm, 28mm, 15mm,
12mm, and varied extension tubes supplied by Ocean Optics (London).
The lenses for the housed Nikons and Pentax were 14mm, 50mm,
60mm; 105mm, 28–200mm zoom, and 70–300mm zoom. Housing
manufacture is by Subal in Austria, Sea & Sea in Japan and Hugyphot
in Switzerland.

Electronic flash was used in virtually all of the underwater photographs and these were supplied by Sea & Sea Ltd. These units were
the YS20, YS50, YS150, YS200, and YS300. For the land cameras, the
Nikon SB24 and SB26 were used. Film stock used was Fujichrome
Velvia, Fujichrome Provia, and Fujichrome RDP. All film processing
was supplied by Expocolour in Edinburgh, Scotland.

Table of Contents

Acknowledgments

This book would have been impossible without the very generous help and support from the Seychelles Ministry of Tourism & Transport. The people from the ministry in the London and Seychelles offices have all been friendly, courteous, and enthusiastic. Special mention must go to Mr. M. J. Loustau-Lalanne, Iqbal Ebrahim, Anne Eibl, Monica Chetty, Liz Lower, and Rose Fayon; Air Seychelles for their support and superb international and inter island services; Glynis Sanders, David Rowat, and the staff of the Seychelles Underwater Centers who have been of immense help and inspiration, and without whose help this guide would not have been possible; Fuji, which supplied all of the film; Sea & Sea of Paignton in Devon, England for underwater lighting; The Shark Group of Amble in Northumberland, England for diving equipment; Adrian Tyte, formerly of Marine Divers International; McCluskey Associates and Judith Greeven for their help and support; and last but not least my wife Lesley, who in addition to being my dive buddy, supports me in my passion to indulge myself in our underwater world, and what better place to do it than in the Seychelles?

Foreword

Many authors and photographers have visited the Seychelles Islands over the years, extolling the Islands' virtues. Now, since the inception of SUBIOS—the Indian Ocean Annual Underwater Film Festival—we have a platform for the world's best underwater photographers to present their work. The Seychelles, though young in political and economic terms, are in fact the tips of an ancient sub-continent and unique in the world.

Lawson Wood has been visiting the islands for over twenty years and is now a regular presenter at SUBIOS, enthralling audiences with his spectacular audio-visual slide show productions. Now he has written the first book to list the most popular diving and snorkeling sites in the Seychelles, lavishly illustrated with his stunning photographs. This book is a concise overview of Seychelles' marine life.

We welcome Lawson as a friend of the Seychelles and feel confident that this book will not only provide some insight into the beauty beneath the waves, it will also encourage many more to sample this beauty for themselves, whether it be from a glass-bottom boat in the St. Anne Marine National Park, snorkeling from one of our many beaches, or by scuba diving from one of the excellent dive centers. With this book we have an opportunity to share the beauty and diversity of the marine life found in our waters. Through Lawson's eyes we have an opportunity to gain a further understanding and appreciation for the marine ecosystem that is essentially Seychelles.

Maurice Loustau-LaLanne
Seychelles Ministry of Tourism and Transport

How to Use This Guide

The purpose of this book is not to be the definitive book on underwater Seychelles, but rather a guide book to acquaint you with some of the varied and most popular dive sites within the main Seychelles group of Mahé, Praslin, and La Digue. It also describes briefly the marine life of those locations and provides enough information to help you decide whether a particular dive site is appropriate to your abilities. The dive sites presented are only a sampling of 35 sites out of the 100 or so registered locations within the main group, notwithstanding the exploratory diving being done by the Seychelles Underwater Center to the outer reaches of the Seychelles Archipelago, the Amirantes, and Aldabra.

St. Anne, Cerf, and Moyenne Islands lie west of the Seychelles capital, Victoria, and St. Anne National Marine Park. Unique animal and plant species make these granite islands popular with terrestrial naturalists and marine biologists. (Photo by Lesley Orson.)

The Seychelles Underwater Center at Beau Vallon Bay on Mahé is a PADI Five-Star Center with a multi-national staff.

The dive-site-by-dive-site descriptions include recommended skill and experience levels, which are explained in the following section. Regardless of whether you read this guide from cover to cover or select topics of interest, certain sections should be regarded as required reading. Safety, buoyancy control, and reef etiquette focus on how to help preserve the fragile marine ecosystem and help you be a more skillful diver.

I have collected information on the dive sites with very specific help from Glynis Sanders and David Rowat of the Seychelles Underwater Center. Although some may consider my choice of sites to be rather arbitrary, it is based on my 20 years' experience of diving around the Seychelles and helping to promote the area in the world diving market.

This guide is directed at active divers who intend to spend a substantial amount of time in the water, but we all need to dry out sometime. The chapters at the beginning of the book on the overview of the islands' history, geography, accommodations, and exploration provide a greater appreciation of what else you can discover among these latter-day Garden of Eden islands.

Divers love the Seychelles warm waters, because they do not need to wear a full wet suit.

The Rating System for Dives and Divers

The rating system for divers in this guide is based on the minimum level of expertise required for each dive (or snorkeling) site. It is considered that a **novice diver** is someone in a reasonable state of physical fitness who has recently completed a basic certification diving course, or a certified diver who has not been diving recently, or who does not have any experience in similar waters. An **intermediate diver** is someone who is a certified diver and in excellent physical condition, has been diving for at least a year following a basic diving certification course, and is experienced in similar waters. An **advanced diver** is considered to be someone who has completed an advanced diving certification course, is in excellent physical condition, and is experienced in similar waters.

As always, divers should assess each dive prior to entering the water and if unsure of the dive details, ask the local dive guide or instructor questions. Dive conditions do vary, even during a dive and divers should be aware of what to do in any given situation. If in any doubt about your diving skill level or conditions with the dive, then contact the operation you are diving with.

1

Overview of the Seychelles

The name alone is exotic and romantic, and conjures up ideas of palm-fringed white sandy beaches, crystal clear waters, coral fringed atolls, and brightly colored tropical fish.

Those imagined thoughts turn out to be a reality when you touch down on Mahé, the main island in the Seychelles Archipelago just 4° south of the equator and more than 1,600 km (1,000 miles) from the east coast of Kenya. Mahé is 27 km long and 8 km wide (16 × 5 miles). There are in fact five main groups, comprising some 115 or so islands with some of the largest coral atolls in the world: Providence; Farquhar; Desroches; Cosmoledo, and the largest of all, Aldabra, which is a World Heritage Site of international importance. Apart from the granite islands—which make up the main group around Mahé, Praslin, La Digue, Aride, Silhouette, Frégate, and their satellites—the coral islands can be split into four distinct groups: The Amirantes, Alphonse, Farquhar, and Aldabra.

The islands form a total land mass of only 445 km^2 (278 mi^2), but they are spread over an exclusive economic zone of more than 1 million km^2 (600,000 mi^2). The granite islands, which only have a land mass of 235 km^2 (146 mi^2), rise majestically from the 75-m (250 ft) deep submarine plateau to over 900 m (3,300 ft) on Morne Seychellois on the main island of Mahé. In contrast, the coral islands of the Seychelles rise only a few meters above the sea and are more like green parks, rather than the lush tropical greenhouses on the main granite islands.

The granite formations on La Digue are famous worldwide and have been used as a backdrop for many movies.

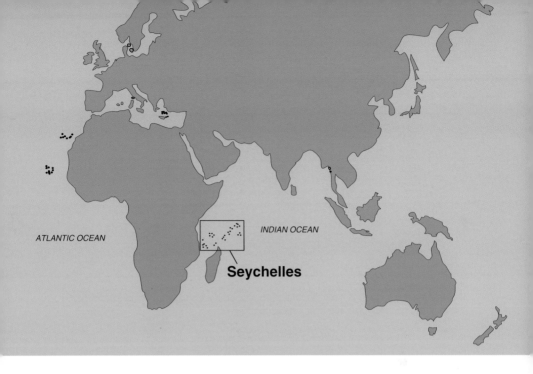

Because it is impossible in a guide such as this to extol the virtues of the other island groups, this book aims at the major tourist islands of Mahé, Praslin, and La Digue in the Seychelles Archipelago. The two outermost islands, Denis and Bird, are the only true coral islands within this group at the edge of the Seychelles Bank; all the other islands in this archipelago are of a granite formation with a surrounding and fringing coral reef.

For travelers who wish to explore the other groups of islands and atolls, Air Seychelles has an island-hopping service which connects from Mahé to most of the group. Desroches in the Amirantes is worthy of note for some superb diving. Aldabra requires special permission, however, several live-aboard boats now travel this area of the Indian Ocean; the diving is regarded by many as some of the most spectacular and interesting of any in the Indian Ocean.

Although the Seychelles are so close to the equator, they do have a varied climate and seasons. These are marked primarily by the shift of the monsoon winds. The southeast monsoon blows from May to the end of October (the dry season) and the northwest from November to April. The wind rarely exceeds 25 kmph (15 mph). The highest rainfall occurs around December and January, with the hottest months being March and April. With temperatures averaging 28°C (82°F) the Seychelles are an ideal vacation (holiday) location.

Mahé is the main island in the group and the hotels are clustered in several small areas, some of which are more open to the climatic weather variations, so it would be prudent to check which hotels are sheltered depending on which time of year that you are planning to visit. The island is cosmopolitan, but with a laid back nature that you soon get used to.

5

Victoria Market, although very popular with tourists, is actually a way of life for the Seychellois, who buy spices, fish, vegetables there.

There is no point being in a hurry anywhere around the island, and why should you?

A short distance northeast from Mahé is the second largest island in the group, **Praslin.** Hailed as the original Garden of Eden by General Gordon (of Khartoum fame), in fact he was referring quite specifically to the Vallée de Mai. This subtropical valley hosts many ancient forest specimens as well as a number of rare and exotic birds including the black parrot with its distinctive cry, and the Seychelles tree frog. The "forbidden fruit," the coco de mer nut, is only found in this valley. The nut strongly resembles the female pelvic region; originally thought to have come from an underwater plant, its true origins were only discovered in 1881. The Vallée de Mai was given the distinction of a World Heritage Site in 1983.

Praslin's sister island of **LaDigue** is like stepping back in time. Transport is by bycicle or ox cart. The island is instantly recognizable from countless advertising campaigns and films. Romance was invented here! These islands are unquestionably photogenic with massive granite boulders interspaced with palm trees just hanging over the edge of the crystal clear blue sea.

The islands' geographical position has also led to a varied and checkered past. The locals, or Seychellois, are a mixture of Indians, European, Asian, and African. Their skin tones range from bronze to ebony and white. The origins are so varied that all classification was abandoned in 1911. This amazing racial mix also accounts for what is in essence a truly relaxed, hospitable atmosphere, where even language takes a side step from French, English, and Creole. Creole is the language of the local people, of the market place, and of the kitchens. Creole cooking is quite unlike anything you have ever tasted.

Flora and Fauna

The Seychelles are all that remain when Africa split away from India in the Pre-Cambrian period. These massive granite submarine upheavals were once part of the supercontinent Pangaea, which was torn apart over 600 million years ago. The Seychelles granite islands are the only islands in the world to be constituted of continental rocks. The main islands have little or no fringing reef for protection and are thought to be the legendary land of Limuria. Bird and Denis Islands, 95 km to the north (60 miles) at the edge of the Seychelles Bank are the only true coral islands in the main group.

Like the Galapagos Islands, their volcanic origin and oceanic isolation has also accounted for a vast number of rare species of animals and plants amid lush vegetation. Many endemic birds, animals, and fish thrive under the protection offered by the numerous terrestrial and marine reserves on and around several of the offshore and isolated islands.

As there are three types of islands in the Seychelles—sand cays, elevated reefs, and granitic islands—there are also three distinct varieties of flora and fauna. There is actually little of interest on the sand cays, which are pan-tropical in origin, but some of the islands, such as Desnoeufs and Bird Island, are major breeding grounds for large numbers of migratory seabirds such as sooty terns, a real ornithological wonder during the breeding season. These islands are also home to large numbers of turtles.

The uplifted reefs are of much greater importance, because they constitute what could be classed as an extension of the vast and diverse ecological systems found on neighboring Madagascar. Aldabra in particular is of the greatest importance due to its size, age, and geographical isolation constituting an ecosystem hardly touched by man. There are more than 150,000 giant land tortoises (compared to only 10,000 in the Galapagos), and it is believed that all may have originated from Madagascar, as well as many endemic birds.

The Seychelles tree frog is extremely rare and found in the national park on Praslin—if you are lucky. (Photo by Lesley Orson.)

The flora and fauna found on the granitic islands of the main group are also of great interest, although much of the original vegetation has been decimated by man. It is interesting to note that due to the varieties of plants and animals found on these islands, the Seychelles are regarded more as the western limit of the distant Oriental Biogeographical Region than that of the closer Ethiopian Region. The endemic species of plants, fish, and animals are unique and although the ancient tortoises and crocodiles were hunted to extinction, there is still so much to enjoy, from the rare pitcher plant (*Nepenthes pervillei*) high up in the Morne Seychellois National Park on Mahé to the Seychelles tree frog (*Megalaxilus seychellensis*) and bronze-eyed gecko (*Aeluronyx seychellensis*) in the Vallée de Mai on Praslin to the Seychelles anemonefish (*Amphiprion fuscocaudatus*) found in the St. Anne Marine National Park. Two nature reserves—Aldabra Atoll and the Vallée de Mai on Praslin Island—have been declared World Heritage Sites by UNESCO.

Seychelles History

The Seychelles Islands were visited over the centuries by Arab traders plying the spice routes between Africa, India, and China who used them for revictualing, which almost wiped out the indigenous population of giant tortoises. Several pirates also used the islands as their base and Astove in particular is rife with stories of lost treasure.

Nestled as they are in the Indian Ocean, over 1,600 km (1,000 miles) from the African coastline of Kenya, the Seychelles escaped human habitation until the early 18th century. From 1506, the Seychelles appreared on Portuguese sailing charts and were known as either the "Seven Sisters" or the "Seven Brothers." At this time Vasco da Gama discovered the Amirantes to the south (originally known as the Admiral's Islands), but it took another hundred years before the islands were fully charted in 1609 on the fourth voyage of the English East India Company, under the command of Alexander Sharpeigh. The company factor, John Jourdain, noted "many cocker nutts, both ripe and greene, of all sorts, and much fishe and fowle and tortells . . . it is a good refreshing place . . . without any feare of danger except the allagartes, for you cannot discern that any people had bene before us."

The English sailed on without planting a flag or annex stone, leaving the islands uninhabited until 1742, when the French governor of Mauritius, Le Vicomte Mahé de Labourdonnais, sent two ships north, led by Lazare Picault to "Abundance Island," later named Mahé. The islands were finally annexed to France in 1756, when Captain Nicholas Morphy placed the Stone of Possession on Mahé; but it was not until 1770, when the first French colonists settled with their African slaves, that man started to make his impression.

Traditional shipbuilding on the Seychelles is still very much a part of local life; the fishing sloops are highly seaworthy.

So far as the naming of the whole group is concerned, it was in honor of Vicomte Moreau des Sechelles, controller general of finance in the French government of Louis XV.

In 1768, Pierre Poivre, adminstrator of the islands of France, mounted an expedition commanded by Marion Dufresne comprising the supply ship *La Digue* and schooner *La Curieuse.* By 1788, the settlements first started around the area of modern-day Victoria were split into about thirty colonies with over two hundred slaves. Monsieur de Malavois introduced the cultivation of spices, cotton oil, wood, and coconuts. In 1791, the colony had 572 inhabitants: 65 white colonists, 20 free blacks, and 487 slaves imported from Africa and Madagascar.

During the French Revolution, the English decided that the Seychelles would be the perfect shipping base between Africa and Ceylon and so began a series of attacks on the Seychelles Islands on May 16, 1794. The French governor at the time, Jean Baptiste Queau de Quinssy, known as the "Father of Seychelles," was obliged to sign the first of a long series of capitulations, which resulted in the islands becoming the property of King George III of England on April 21, 1811. The islands were finally cecedied along with Mauritius to Britain following the Treaty of Paris on May 30, 1814.

The population gradually grew and by 1835, when the abolishment of slavery in the Seychelles was voted by the British Parliament, there were

State House in Victoria, residence of the President, Mr. France Albert Rene. (Photo by Lesley Orson.)

7,500 inhabitants, of which 6,521 were originally slaves. This spelled the decline of the huge plantations. Share-cropping started and there were now new categories of fishermen, artisans, and farmers. Unavoidably, the population started to disperse to other islands including Mauritius, and by 1840, the population had shrunk to 5,500.

When the Suez Canal opened on November 17, 1869, the Seychelles were the natural stopover for ships plying the trade routes between eastern Africa, Mauritius, and Europe. That, together with the production of vanilla and coconut oil, soon became the Seychelles most important export. Administration on the islands was still based in Mauritius, and it soon became obvious that this type of tutelage was no longer acceptable.

On August 31, 1903, the Seychelles were given the status of British Crown Colony by Edward VII, separate from Mauritius. In that same year, the clock tower in Victoria (a scale replica of the clock tower in Vauxhall Bridge Road, London) was inaugurated and well known because it rings twice, once to tell you the time, the second just in case you did not hear it the first time!

Copra, cinnamon, patchouli, and citronella essences soon gained popularity, and by 1939, times were changing. The Second World War saw the Seychelles as being extremely important for the Royal Navy due to their strategic position in the Indian Ocean. From July 1945, the Labour Government newly appointed Governor Percy Selwyn Clarke launched a program of social reforms; unfortunately, the only electorate were the tax payers who represented around 10% of the population.

In 1964, the president of the Seychelles, a young lawyer named France Albert Rene, founded the Seychelles People's United Party (SPUP), which fought against colonial power and sought a constitution supporting the liberation of the Seychelles. At the same time the Seychelles Democratic Party was founded, which supported the integration of the Seychelles with Great Britain. A constitutional conference was held in London in 1970 and transformed the council into a legislative assembly, and by 1975, the Seychelles became an "autonomous colony."

On June 29, 1976, the Seychelles Republic was born with a coalition government led by James Mancham. The Seychelles finally became an autonomous nation on June 5, 1977 following a coup d'état installing a single party state with Mr. France Albert Rene as president of the republic. Following political changes worldwide, there are now multi-party elections and a new constitution. Seychelles is currently an independent republic within the British Commonwealth.

Seychelles Today

Today, the Republic of Seychelles is an independent, non-aligned nation with a unique culture and combination of ethnic affinities. The egalitarian education system is aimed at developing human resources to correspond with the country's needs, and the local Creole language is now taught in the schools. The greatest rise in the socio-economic growth has been the tourist industry. Supported by the World Bank and the European Economic Community, massive investment has been injected into the islands, the first real bank opened its doors in 1959, and the first airport on Mahé (in 1971) resulted in the rapid growth that made the Seychelles one of the top vacation (holiday) destinations in the world.

The population of the Seychelles is now around 70,000; the only town (and capital) Victoria and her suburbs have some 25,000 souls. Victoria is nestled at the foot of a rampart-like mountain range, hidden under a mass of greenery and is now one of the most modern capital cities among the Indian Ocean islands.

The Victoria Clock, erected in 1903, is a scale model of the clock tower in Vauxhall Bridge Road, London. The clock is well known because it rings twice, once to tell you the time, the second just in case you did not hear it the first time!

You do not need to look far to discover the Seychelles roots, however; the capital of Victoria still has its open market each Saturday; and yes, it is interesting to us tourists, but market day is a way of life to the Seychellois. Victoria is clean and friendly and with such a mixture of buildings and architecture that you wonder where you are sometimes. Dotted around the main island of Mahé are about 25 small villages that are grouped around their church, school, police station, and political party centers, and all face the sea. As you travel over the central massif, you come across tea plantations, stepped into the hillside and often shrouded in low clouds or fog over the rainforest.

The villages not only have kept their old world charm, they have also retained their original picturesque French names: Port Glaud, Bel Ombre, Anse Forbans, Quatre Bornes, Glacis, etc. Here you can watch traditional shipbuilders at work or view the local handicraft industries. Tradition lies heavy in the Seychelles, but in stark contrast the Seychellois have also grasped the latest technology and the republic is gaining in strength and popularity each year.

As well as hosting the Indian Ocean Athletics Games and world-class sea angling festivals, the Seychelles are also home to SUBIOS—the annual Indian Ocean Underwater Film Festival, where the world's top underwater photographers present their latest work to an enthralled captive audience. On site underwater photographic competitions also take place amid lectures and seminars on conservation aspects about the Seychelles and the Indian Ocean marine ecosystems.

How to Get There

We no longer have to take the slow ferry from Aden en route to Mauritius; there are now several weekly international flights from London, Paris, Frankfurt, Zurich, Rome, Singapore, Johannesburg, Nairobi, Madrid, Dubai, Bombay, Manchester, and Tel Aviv. Air Seychelles is perhaps the most popular of the airline companies and has a reputation of excellent service within the industry. There are flights two times each week from London Gatwick. On Sundays the flight routes are via Rome and on Wednesdays via Paris. One weekly flight leaves Manchester via Zurich, as well as from Frankfurt non-stop on a Friday; Paris on Wednesday; Tel Aviv on Tuesday; Rome on Sunday; and Zurich on Saturday.

In addition to these flights, British Airways also offers a non-stop flight from London on Wednesday and Sunday. Air France also flies direct and there is now a budget flight on Aeroflot from Moscow. Kenya Airways also operates from the African mainland.

Air Seychelles, which operates the inter-island service is recorded in the *Guinness Book of Records* as the world's smallest international airline; yet, it still managed to service three continents and handle 46% of the passengers visiting the Seychelles. To protect and preserve the unique and

Victoria Harbor and marina are quite "sleepy" and very picturesque.

The Air Seychelles inter island airplanes are named after each of the small outer islands they visit. This plane is the Isle of Desroches.

precious environment of the Seychelles, the total number of visitors is limited to 150,000 per year.

Live-aboard dive boats also sail around the islands, and although most pick up passengers from Mahé, it is possible to fly first to Kenya or South Africa and then onwards to the Seychelles, thus being able to perhaps have a land safari on an African game reserve and then onto the Seychelles for the second part of your vacation.

Island Hopping

Each of the Seychelles Islands has something different to offer and you should include two or more islands in your itinerary to experience as much of the Seychelles as possible. You will not be disappointed.

Mahé is the largest of the islands and in many ways perhaps the most spectacular, with its massive granite peaks, tropical, lush vegetation, superb beaches, and Victoria, the capital city of the Seychelles.

Praslin, apart from its fabulous beaches, is perhaps best known for the Vallée de Mai World Heritage Site, where the Coco de Mer palm and several endemic wild animals are found.

La Digue is justifiably famous for its fabulous granite boulder rock formations that jut out into the sea, its ox-cart tours, and paradise flycatcher bird sanctuary.

Bird, on the edge of the Seychelles Bank, has more than one million nesting sooty terns from May to October and has the heaviest tortoise in the world—Esmeralda.

Denis is also out on the Seychelles bank and is the only other coral island in the main group. It has superb snorkeling and diving.

Frégate is home to the rare Seychelles magpie robin and the flightless giant tenebrionid beetle. With five beaches it is a dream destination.

Silhouette is reputed to have been home to a notorious pirate whose treasure is still hidden somewhere on the island.

Desroches is surrounded by 80 km (50 miles) of reefs just waiting to be explored; September to May is the best time.

Cousin is owned by the Royal Society for Nature Conservation and is administered by the International Council of Bird Preservation. Visitors are limited to 20 and then only on 3 days each week.

Aride is home to the greatest concentration of seabirds in the central region and boasts the world's largest number of breeding lesser noddy and roseate terns. The island is also owned by the Royal Society for Nature Conservation.

Curieuse and the area that surrounds it is a marine national park and home to giant tortoise brought from Aldabra.

Chauve Souris in the Cote d'Or on Praslin can be rented by private groups and is idyllic.

Felicité is also available to be rented privately for two weeks at a time.

Parasailing on Beau Vallon Bay is just one of the many popular pastimes for tourists to this superb beach.

Aldabra, located 1,150 km (715 miles) southwest of Mahé, comprises three magnificent atolls and one platform reef. It is arguably the least touched by man in the Indian Ocean. The main atoll is so huge that you cannot see from one side to the other; all of the Seychelles main islands' group could fit snugly within its lagoon.

Practical Information

Hotels. The Seychelles are a true island paradise, unspoiled by commercialism, but you need not worry about the standard of accommodation. Most hotels are to the highest of modern international standards with full air-conditioning, private bathrooms, swimming pools, and sports facilities. There are also the much smaller and quainter guest houses where the old-world standards of former plantation houses are now unsurpassed for peace, privacy, and superb cuisine. Although there are no true night clubs, traditional Sega dancing and barbeques are more the norm with local folk and modern live music. A couple of the hotels also host world-class Casinos for those who enjoy the gaming tables.

The Coral Strand Hotel is particularly popular with guests on Beau Vallon Bay; the Seychelles Underwater Center is located in this hotel.

Foreign Exchange and Banks. The currency unit is the Seychelles rupee (SR), which is divided into 100 cents. There is no preference for currency to exchange; all are welcome and can be exchanged at most hotels or at any of the local banks. The exchange is a fixed rate, but it can fluctuate. Credit cards are accepted, i.e., American Express, Diners Club, Barclaycard, Visa, Access, Mastercard.

The Seychelles Savings Bank, branches of Barclays Bank International, Banque Francaise Commerciale, Bank of Baroda, and Habib Bank will all exchange foreign currency and travelers' checks. Banks at the airport are always open for arrivals and departures of international flights. Most of the international hotels will also exchange your currency at the same rate as that of the banks.

Transportation. At last count there were 26 car rental companies on the main island of Mahé and 6 on Praslin. The main mode of tourist transport is in either Suzuki Jeeps or Mini-Mokes. These are ideal for lugging your dive gear around in, but offer no security whatsoever. Modern sedans are also available and these are the preferred choice when traveling farther afield. Although there is very little crime on the islands, unnecessary risks should not be taken. Your tour operator can arrange your transportation before you leave your home country, but I recommend that you arrange everything after you arrive on the island as it will cost less and you will be able to inspect the vehicle of your choice.

Buses are another alternative to getting around the islands and are very cheap compared to taxi fares. When on La Digue, the only form of transport is by ox-cart or bicycle! Yachts are also available for charter from Victoria Marina and you will be able to visit the outer islands at your

16

The Seychelles Yacht Club, situated within the Victoria marina, is very popular. Visiting yachtsmen and local captains can be found here as well as information on chartering a yacht.

leisure. Glass-bottomed boats, of course, will allow you to see the wonders of the St. Anne Marine National Park without getting your feet wet. Ferries operate regularly between the nearby islands and Air Seychelles offers an island-hopping service that is reasonably priced. There is also a helicopter service to Silhouette and Praslin as well as island sight-seeing tours. Contact Helicopter Seychelles, PO Box 595, Seychelles International Airport. Tel: (248) 375277.

Entry Requirements. You must have a valid passport to enter the Seychelles and onward or return air tickets, accommodations, and sufficient funds for your stay. Camping is not allowed. Visas are not normally required and a one month's visitor's pass is issued by the immigration authorities on arrival. This may be renewed for up to three months free of charge.

Time Difference. The Seychelles are 4 hours ahead of GMT or 3 hours ahead of Central European Time in winter and 2 hours in summer.

Medical Facilities. Visitors may obtain emergency treatment under the National Medical Service for illness and accident at the basic consultation fee. Prescribed medicines and drugs can be bought at the hospital pharmacy or from some pharmacists (chemists). Most of the smaller district villages have a clinic. There is a two-person portable recompression chamber at Victoria Hospital available for use in emergency only. The nearest full hyperbaric recompression facilities are in Mombassa, Kenya. It is imperative that whenever you travel overseas, you must have a more than adequate health insurance policy. Insurances should also cover loss of luggage, theft, accident, and cancellation.

Postal Services. The main post office is in Victoria, near the Clock Tower. Airmail collections are at 3pm on weekdays and at noon on Saturdays. All Seychelles postal addresses have a post-office box at the post office.

Voltages. Electrical current is 240 volts AC, 50Hz. Plugs are square pin, three-point, the same as in the UK. Twin-point shaver-style adapters are available in the bathrooms in the major hotels, but for those requiring 110 volts for recharging their lamps or strobes, it would be better to take an adapter with you or contact the particular diving operation that you are staying with to see if they are able to help.

What to Wear. Women should wear light cotton dresses, slacks, and shorts at any time of the year. Formal dress is seldom worn in the evening. Topless sunbathing is allowed on the major beaches, but discretion should be taken when among locals. For men, lightweight slacks or shorts and open neck shirts are perfect, as are shirts and slacks for evening wear. When visiting Victoria or entering restaurants, shops, banks and post office, swim wear should NOT be worn. Be aware of the sensitivity of the locals.

Water Wear. You only require a swimsuit when in the sea due to the almost constant water temperature all year round, even at depth. However, it's recommended that you wear either a lycra skin-suit or thin wet suit for diving and snorkeling to protect you against coral abrasions and stings from those unseen planktonic beasties in the water, as well as the fierce

The restaurant of the Paradise Sun Hotel on Praslin is spacious and offers first-class cuisine.

sun while on the surface. Topless bathing is permitted on the more popular beaches, but discretion should be taken when among locals.

Photographic Tips. When loading film into your camera, beware of cool air-conditioned apartments. When you take the camera outside, the increase in temperature will cause the inside to condensate. Similarly, try not to leave your camera out in the sun, because when you take it underwater, the decrease in water temperature will also cause condensation to appear on the inside of the lens or inside of a housing's port.

Tips for Service. Tips are NOT expected in the Seychelles. All hotels and restaurant tariffs include service, but, as always, extra tipping is at your discretion.

Turtle Products. Some turtle products are sold in a few of the islands' souvenir stalls at the side of the main street in Victoria. Due to the CITES law (Convention on International Trade for Endangered Species) enacted in 1978 by the US government, visitors from the US and Europe are prohibited from taking home any sea turtle products, nor will the US Customs authorities permit the transshipment of any turtle products through any type of US port.

Suntanning. Each year, thousands of tourists visit the Seychelles with the idea of going home with a suntan. However, many get burnt on their first day and spend a very sore and uncomfortable few days recovering, ruining their vacation. It is recommended to plan your sunbathing in the following way if you are not used to the strength of the sun's rays:

1st day—10 minutes; 2nd day—15 minutes; 3rd day—25 minutes; 4th day—35 minutes; 5th day—50 minutes; 6th day—75 minutes.

Keep yourself and your children well protected with a high factor of sun screen and pay particular attention to the top of the head (wear a hat), the nose, backs of legs, (especially when snorkeling) and the tops of feet.

Botanical Gardens. The Botanical Gardens on Mahé are close to Victoria and cover 15 acres. They are pleasantly mature, having been laid out in 1901 by Rivaltz Dupont. There is a kiosk detailing the different flora and fauna to be found.

National Parks and Reserves. Of the total land mass of the Seychelles, 46% has been designated as national parks, reserves, or protected areas. A further 140 km^2 (90 mi^2) has been designated as marine national parks for the conservation of important marine ecosystems. All of the national nature reserves are able to be visited on foot or by boat,

Windsurfing and other watersports are available on Beau Vallon Beach.

and many have some breathtaking walks and hikes through semi-tropical jungle.

Sailing. There is an impressive variety of charter vessels available from Victoria Marina, from luxury yachts to catamarans, to sail around the Seychelles Islands in unadulterated luxury.

Fishing. A sport still relatively new to the Seychelles, there are now specific charter boats that travel to the outer islands of the group to catch marlin, kingfish, sailfish, and tuna. An international fishing festival is held each year during April.

Golf. There is a non-professional 9-hole golf course at the Reef Hotel Golf Club for those who need a break from all of the water!

Seychelles Cuisine. When it comes to food, even the fussiest of gourmets should be able to find dishes to their delight. As well as the local Creole cuisine, there is Chinese, Indian, French, and Japanese. Creole is a blend of fruit, fish, vegetables, and spices.

Driving in Seychelles. Driving is on the left. A valid driving license must be presented and all drivers must be over 21 years of age. Most cars are hired on third-party insurance and for full comprehensive insurance, an extra premium will be levied. Cars and Jeeps are available on Mahé and Praslin only.

Craft Village. About 14 km (9 miles) south of Victoria on Mahé, the craft village comprises various workshops where artisans can be seen at work and local crafts can be bought. There is a restaurant, a traditional colonial house and a coconut museum.

Weddings in Paradise. Why not get married in the Seychelles! For foreign citizens, the ceremony is recognized under International Law, conducted by the registrar at the hotel on Mahé, Praslin, and La Digue. Couples should be in residence for 11 days before the ceremony, be over 18 years of age, and must travel with the appropriate original documents (birth certificate, if applicable; decree absolute, if widowed; marriage and death certificate and legal proof of name change, if applicable). All foreign documents must have an official English translation verified by the appropriate embassy. For further details, contact: The Registrar, Civil Status Office, PO Box 430, Victoria, Mahé, Seychelles.

Weddings in paradise are becoming more popular. What better place to get married than on a beach in the middle of the Indian Ocean?

Weather. The climate is tropical, mostly equable, as the surrounding ocean has a moderating effect. The Seychelles are outside of the Cyclone Belt so high winds and thunderstorms are rare. Even though the Seychelles are so close to the equator, they do have a varied climate and seasons. These are marked primarily by the shift of the monsoon winds. The southeast monsoon blows from mid-May to the end of October (the dry season); and the northwest from November to April, although the wind rarely exceeds 25kmph (15mph). The highest rainfall occurs around December and January, with the hottest months being March and April. With temperatures averaging 28°C (82°F) the Seychelles are an ideal holiday location.

For divers the best underwater visibility and calmest seas are from April to May and October to November. However, the visibility can drop dramatically during November with the rise in the plankton, which sweeps across the Indian Ocean, bringing with it manta rays and whale sharks. Conditions are normally good throughout the rest of the year, and dive sites are chosen according to the prevailing winds to allow for the best conditions.

The outer islands are more susceptible to offshore winds and, of course, the might of the Indian Ocean swell, which can travel a long way fueled by some distant cyclone. However, visibility is generally always better and the water invariably has that translucent "blue" quality. Tidal variations and current can be punishing to say the least, and the exposed tips of the headlands where small isolated islands lie, such as L'Ilot on Mahé, can present unexpected difficulties. On one particular dive, photographing in the mid channel between L'Ilot and the mainland, we were hit by what can only be described as an underwater squall. The current increased dramatically and the underwater visibility reduced to only a couple of meters in as many minutes. Riding out the storm, it cleared after another ten minutes and we continued our dive in calm and peaceful conditions.

◄ *My wife Lesley drops down through a shaft in the reef on one of the Seychelles' outer islands.*

2

Diving in the Seychelles

With over 900 species of fish, 100 types of shells, and 50 varieties of coral, the Seychelles are a scuba diver's paradise and an underwater photographer's dream. There is little or no current around the islands, lots of fish, colorful corals, and the above-average chance of seeing large pelagics such as turtles, manta rays, marlin, and whale sharks. Most dive sites are just a 10–20-minute boat ride from the shore opposite and dive centers such as the Seychelles Underwater Center offer free transport from your hotel. All of the dive centers on Mahé, Praslin, and La Digue offer services of the highest standards.

The Seychelles Underwater Center now operates the largest number of centers and is regarded by many as one of the top diving organizations in the Indian Ocean. They are a dedicated Five Star PADI center with a multilingual staff. With over 20 years' experience in the industry, the full range of certification courses are offered in German, French, Italian, Eng-

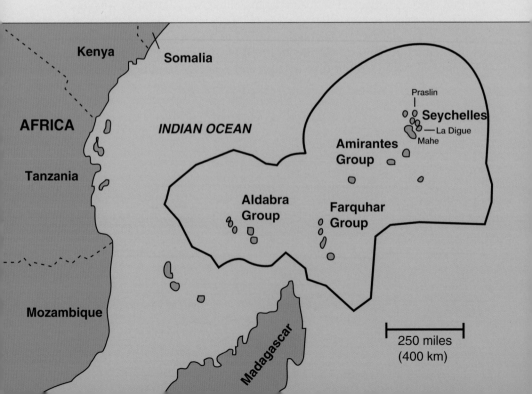

lish, and other languages. Whether you want to try scuba diving for the first time, gain an international diving certificate, or wish to expand your diving horizons, then the Seychelles are definitely the place to be.

You might want to take an underwater photography course and attend the SUBIOS Film Festival and Photographic Shoot-out Competition. Details of the SUBIOS competition can be obtained from the Seychelles Tourist Office, 2nd floor, Eros House, 111 Baker Street, London, UK, tel 44 (0) 171 224 1670, fax 44 (0) 171 486 1352; or from the competition organizer, SUBIOS, PO Box 384, Victoria, Republic of Seychelles. The Seychelles Ministry of Tourism & Transport, Independence House, PO Box 92, Republic of Seychelles, tel (00) 248 225314, fax: (00) 248 224035.

Dive Site Terminology

Pinnacle or bommie—a large coral head, tower-shaped, sometimes also referred to as a *patch reef.*

Canyon—a slice in the coral reef or between granite boulders.

Tunnel—sometimes known as swim-throughs, ravines, or crevices, this is a hole running through the reef or under granite rock.

Shelf—where the deep water begins.

Wall or Drop-off—the reef that forms the shelf or a *mini-wall,* which is the side of a huge granite boulder.

Sand chute—a deep gulley that connects the *sand plane* above the reef to the depths below; this only occurs in very deep waters off the edge of the continental shelf.

The Seychelles Underwater Center's Reef Diver II *returns to shore after another successful dive.*

3

Mahé Dive Sites

These dive sites, primarily of granite rock in origin, are heavily encrusted by rich marine growth and populated by the typical fish and invertebrate species of the Indian Ocean. The island's oceanic isolation has

Dive Site Ratings	Novice	Intermediate	Advanced
1 *Ennerdale* Wreck		x	x
2 Brissaire Rocks		x	x
3 Shark Bank			x
4 L'Ilot	x	x	x
5 Chuckles Rocks	x	x	x
6 Vista Bay Rocks*	x	x	x
7 Sunset Rocks*	x	x	x
8 Beau Vallon Reef	x	x	x
9 Aquarium	x	x	x
10 Twin Barges & Corsair Reef	x	x	x
11 *Auberge* Wreck		x	x
12 Danzille*	x	x	x
13 Whale Rock*	x	x	x
14 Baie Ternay Point		x	x
15 Baie Ternay Marine Park*	x	x	x
16 Lighthouse		x	x
17 Conception Point*		x	x
18 Trois Bancs			x
19 Ile Therese*	x	x	x
20 Iles aux Vaches*		x	x
21 One Tree Island		x	x
22 Intendance Rocks		x	x
23 The Reef*	x	x	x
24 St. Anne Marine National Park Beacon Island*	x	x	x

*Excellent snorkeling

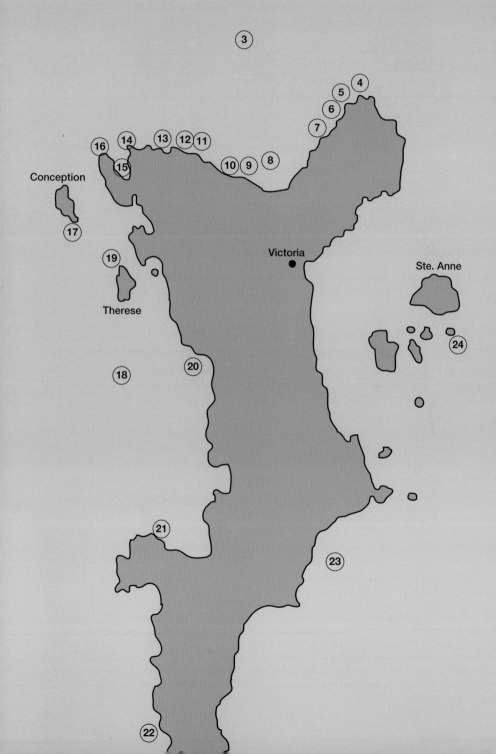

Mahe

Conception

Victoria

Ste. Anne

Therese

The Seychelles anemonefish (Amphiprion fuscocaudatus) *is commonly found on many anemones on the inshore reefs.*

accounted for many indigenous species unique to Seychelles waters, such as the Seychelles anemonefish (*Amphiprion fuscocaudatus*). Although the soft corals are much smaller and more of a dwarf variation of those found in the Red Sea or in Malaysia, they are very brightly colored and are home to some amazing forms of marine life.

Diving around Mahé can be seasonal, and it is always better to check with your tour operator, or contact the dive centers personally to check out which areas are to be dived, what the prevailing water and weather conditions are, and which dive sites are on the agenda. You may wish to visit Mahé to coincide with the whale sharks and the SUBIOS Film Festival, or you may wish to laze around during the hottest months. Mahé is particularly interesting and should be sampled over all of the seasons as there are always lee shores and sheltered conditions.

There are three dives that are classed as long-range adventure dive sites and involve travel time of more than 45 minutes. Divers should preferably be of an advanced qualification: These are Brissaire Rocks, Shark Bank and the *Ennerdale* wreck.

Ennerdale Wreck 1

Expertise Required:	Intermediate to Advanced
Location:	45-minute boat ride northeast from Beau Vallon Bay
Typical Depth Range:	20–30 m (66–100 ft)
Typical Current Conditions:	Slight to moderate, can be choppy on surface
Access:	By dive boat only

The *Ennerdale* was a British Royal Navy Fleet Auxilliary motor tanker, owned by the Anglo-Norness Shipping Co. Ltd. Originally built by Liel-er Howaldtswerke AG in Kiel in 1963, she was chartered to the Royal Fleet Auxiliary RFA in 1967. Weighing 29,189 tons, she was 710 ft long by 98.5 ft wide, had a top speed of 15.5 knots, and was loaded with 41,500 tons of refined furnace oil and gasoil to supply H.M. Frigate *Andromeda*. The *Ennerdale's* service with the RFA lasted for only three years, ending when she sank on a sandbank after striking an unchartered rock, badly holing her starboard side, seven miles from Port Victoria on June 1, 1970.

The wreck of the Ennerdale *is now well broken up in 30 m of water (100 ft) and is a particular favorite with visiting divers.*

The lionfish (Pterois volitans) *is commonly found amid the wreckage of the* Ennerdale *and is quite approachable, despite its reputation.*

The *Ennerdale's* 18 British officers and 42 seamen from the Seychelles all abandoned safely from the vessel from which the oil was leaking badly. Being a navigation hazard, the wreck was subsequently reported to be bombed and totally demolished by H.M. Submarine *Cachalot* after the oil slick had been cleared by the Royal Navy.

She now lies in three sections in 30 m of water, and dives tend to be around the stern section where the ship is mostly intact with the wheel-house and propellor readily accessible. The rest of the ship, however, is largely broken up with the main part of the superstructure being quite open and slowly undergoing colonization by small growths of soft and hard corals, with fire coral in abundance on some of the upper sections. As you descend to the ship, the water column soon becomes crowded with large schools of batfish (*Platax tiera*), which will follow you about on the entire dive.

The crumpled bows tend to have a congregation of stingrays and small white-tipped reef sharks, but these soon head off into the blue as you approach them. The tangled superstructure is quite interesting and with it being quite open, it allows for relatively safe exploration. Due to the depth limitations of the wreck, it is better to swim back towards the stern which is home to numerous moray eels, schools of batfish, and golden snapper, that vie for your attention. From here it is a safe and easy access up the mooring line to the awaiting dive boat.

Expertise Required:	Intermediate to advanced
Location:	Northeast of L'Ilot to two small groups of rocks
Typical Depth Range:	10–20 m (33–66 ft)
Typical Current Conditions:	Moderate to strong
Access:	By dive boat only

Brissaire Rocks are virtually smothered in fire coral, and these exposed offshore pinnacles are home to countless species of fish, as well as eagle rays and huge Napoleon wrasse (*Cheilinus undulatus*). The second set of rocks about 30 m due east (100 ft) are known as the Dragon's Teeth due to their sharp points only being visible when the sea is rough and the surge breaks over them. Both locations can be seen on the same dive, but the swim can be quite arduous, particularly when the tide is running. More often than not, the current can be quite strong through this exposed site, and there is also generally surge to contend with, particularly during the winter months, so additional care should be taken with your bouyancy and position in the water column to avoid crashing into the coral.

Fire coral (Millepora dichotoma) *is very common on Brissaire Rocks, covering large expanses of the shallower granite boulders.*

Reef whitetip sharks are commonly found at Brissaire Rocks resting under coral ledges and granite boulders. They are no threat to divers.

The reef is made up of large granite blocks covered in soft and hard corals; the nooks and crannies, large swim-throughs and overhanging arches are teeming with fish life and regular sightings of nurse sharks and reef whitetip sharks make this area a popular destination. Schools of wrasse and parrotfish intermingle with snapper, grouper, and huge numbers of chromis and fusiliers. There are also large stands of staghorn coral (*Acropora sp.*) where sweetlips and squirrelfish hide in the shadows. This is an excellent dive site and should not be missed.

Expertise Required:	Advanced
Location:	8 km (5 mi) northwest from Beau Vallon Bay
Typical Depth Range:	30 m (100 ft)
Typical Current Conditions:	Moderate to strong
Access:	By dive boat only

Reputed to be the best dive site off the west coast of Mahé, Shark Bank is a massive granite pillar plateau that rises from 30 m (100 ft) with several massive granite boulders on top. Situated over 8 km (5 miles) from Beau Vallon Bay, this pinnacle is a natural focus teeming with fish life not normally associated with the mainland. As the name implies, sharks are quite often seen in the area, but large stingrays are more commonly seen around the boulder outcrops. The walls are covered with bright orange sponges and white gorgonians. Large pelagics are generally seen here due to the strong tidal streams. There is nearly always current present on this site, so it is best to try and reach the seabed as quickly as possible and stay nearby the mooring line for additional safety.

The giant stingray (Himantura granulata) *is seen on most dives at Shark Bank due to the isolation of this offshore plateau.*

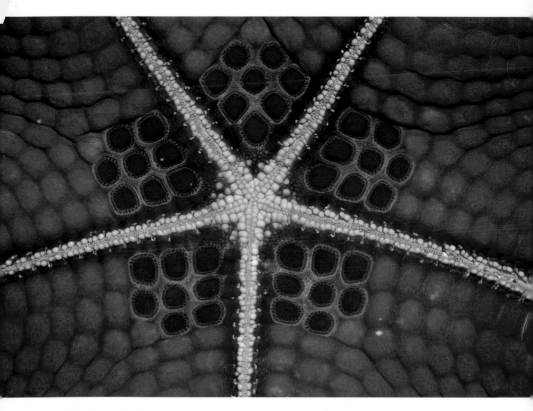

This close-up of the underside of the pincushion sea urchin shows the beautiful natural coloration of these largely ignored, but quite common, echinoderms.

Pincushion starfish are common (*Cultica novaeguineae*) and always have a symbiotic shrimp that lives on the shell. Cowfish (*Lactoria fornasini*) are also common and rarely seen on the mainland. Looking closely at the pinkish white gorgonian sea fans you may also come across small spider crabs or even sea slugs or nudibranchs. Unfortunately, the time at this depth limits exploration, which is why I go back time after time. This is a highly recommended site but for *experienced divers only.*

L'Ilot 4

Expertise Required:	Novice
Location:	Small Islet at the northwestern tip of Mahé
Typical Depth Range:	6–16 m (20–52 ft)
Typical Current Conditions:	Light to Moderate
Access:	By dive boat only

This is definitely my favorite dive on Mahé and ranks at the top of the list on most of the other island's near-shore dive sites. Although this is an off-shore boat dive, I have included it in the novice category because it is just so good, under the right conditions. It is often the case that even advanced divers are unable to dive the site when the tide is particularly fierce.

L'Ilot is one of the most spectacular dive sites at the exposed tip of Beau Vallon Bay at North Point. This tiny granite outcrop of several large granite boulders has formed an islet topped by a couple of palm trees. This site is bursting with marine life: tubastrea, the golden cup coral, festooning the canyons and gulleys, gorgonians or sea fans and other soft corals abound. On one night dive at L'Ilot, we found three Spanish dancer nudibranchs all with symbiotic shrimps within one meter of each other. Yellowspotted burrfish (*Chilomycterus spilostylus*) are always seen on the dive as well as numerous anemones and clownfish.

Between the small island and the mainland, the current can be quite strong, but the small cluster of boulders in the center yields one of the highest densities of life I have seen anywhere. Small peppered moray eels (*Siderea grisea*) live in harmony with literally thousands of hingeback shrimps (*Rhynchocinetes rugulosus*). An excellent dive.

The golden cup coral (Tubastrea aurea) covers most of the available rock surfaces and mini walls. The polyps only extend at night to feed on the plankton.

Expertise Required:	Novice
Location:	Southwest of L'Ilot in same offshore chain of granite boulders, but do not break the surface
Typical Depth Range:	10–15 m (33–50 ft)
Typical Current Conditions:	Moderate
Access:	By dive boat only

This site is a long expanse of low-lying and overlapping granite boulders with the more sheltered or inshore side covered in dwarf soft corals and pinkish white gorgonian sea fans. Under the crevices you can find small groups of hatchetfish (*Pempheris oualensis*) amid golden cup corals. These tumbled granite boulders hold an enormous amount of shade-loving fish and you can study cleaning stations at your leisure all over this location.

You should be able to see the bearded scorpionfish (*Scorpaenopsis barbata*) amid some of the soft corals. The spotfin lionfish (*Pterois antennata*) is also evident as well as the spiny lobster (*Panulirus versicolor*). It is between Chuckles Rocks and L'Ilot that whale sharks congregate in the winter. November in particular is renowned for whale shark sightings and most divers at that time of year will experience that chance of a lifetime to snorkel and dive with the largest fish in the ocean.

Longnosed filefish (Oxymonacanthus longirostris) are commonly found among the small stands of Aropora coral.

◄ *This peppered moray eel (Siderea grisea) lives at L'Ilot in a coral enclave with literally hundreds of cleaning shrimps.*

Expertise Required: Novice
Location: Directly opposite the Vista Bay Hotel
Typical Depth Range: 10–15 m (33–50 ft)
Typical Current Conditions: Slight to Moderate
Access: By dive boat only

Although the dive on this massive granite boulder is primarily a boat dive, there is also excellent snorkeling close to the shore and directly out from the hotel. There are always lots of fish including wrasse, parrotfish, and sergeant majors. The granite boulder is steeply sided and covered in a variety of soft corals and golden cup corals. Murex shells (*Chicoreus microphyllus*) can be found around these golden cup corals and assume the same coloration. The most common anemonefish found here is the skunk anemonefish (*Amphiprion akallopisos*) and is associated with the magnificent anemone (*Heteractis magnifica*). If you look closely at these anemones, you should also be able to spot small cleaner shrimp and the anemone crab (*Neopetrolisthes oshimai*), which also lives with immunity amid the anemone's stinging cells. Look out for a parasitic amphipod (*Lironeca sp.*), which attaches itself on the head and around the gills of the fish. This is a common sight in Seychelles' waters.

Spiny lobster under large granite boulders are a common sight on most dives.

Expertise Required:	Novice
Location:	Opposite the Sunset Hotel
Typical Depth Range:	3–10 m (10–33 ft)
Typical Current Conditions:	Slight
Access:	From the shore or by dive boat

This long series of granite boulders stretches well out perpendicular to the shore forming numerous gullies and canyons. For the most part, the rocks have steep sides and the numerous gulleys have profuse growths of small fan and soft corals. This is a popular location for spotting lionfish and scorpionfish.

Sunset is also a very popular location for night diving, but care must be taken amid the shallower reef areas due to the concentrations of fragile corals and long-spined sea urchins (*Diadema setosum*). There is also a small species of shrimp (*Stegopontonia commensalis*) that lives amid these dangerous spines and generally are only seen when you examine each sea urchin with a strong dive light. Moray eels are common as well as numerous other species of shrimps and crabs.

Small gorgonian fan corals extend their polyps to collect plankton. This fan coral is covered in tiny yellow brittle starfish.

Expertise Required:	Novice
Location:	Close to Beau Vallon Beach
Typical Depth Range:	12–20 m (40–66 ft)
Typical Current Conditions:	Slight
Access:	By dive boat only

This reef is a low coral formation reef of primarily staghorn and leather corals.There are several small coral bommies surrounded by a flat sandy seabed, where on closer inspection you should be able to see the interaction between the shrimp and gobies that live in burrows in the sand.

Juveniles of many reef fish are found all over these coral heads including wrasse and parrotfish. Anemonefish and symbiotic crabs can be found on large anemones, and moray eels are seen on almost every dive. During the summer months, turtles have also been known to frequent the area.

Being near the dive centers along Beau Vallon Bay, it is a popular site with beginners and fish watchers and is regularly visited by the dive stores during scuba instruction courses.

The spotted anemone crab (Neopetrolisthes maculatus) *associates with many anemones, generally clinging to the undersides, or walking among the tentacles with immunity.*

Expertise Required: Novice
Location: Close to Beau Vallon Beach
Typical Depth Range: 5–14 m (16–45 ft)
Typical Current Conditions: Slight
Access: By dive boat only

Well named, this dive site is quite similar in structure to Beau Vallon Reef (Dive Site No. 8) but instead of numerous small coral bommies, this reef is made up of two quite large distinct coral formations surrounded by sand. A popular destination with students, this is one of those locations where someone diving for the first time will get a taste of diving in the Seychelles. There are good stands of coral, anemones and clownfish, moray eels, and numerous species of parrotfish and wrasse. Batfish and sergeant majors are common in the water column as you approach the reef. Angelfish can always be seen scouting the reef in their lifelong mating pairs, as well as butterflyfish and numerous groupers.

The fimbriated moray eel is quite common on all of the Seychelles reefs and is an active feeder at night.

Expertise Required:	Novice
Location:	East of Beau Vallon Bay, almost opposite the Fisherman's Cove Hotel
Typical Depth Range:	6–25 m (20–80 ft)
Typical Current Conditions:	Slight to moderate
Access:	By dive boat only

This is a superb site and combines two barges and an excellent shallow coral reef if you stay too long at depth. The barges—each 18 m long (60 ft) were sunk deliberately in 1989 as part of an ongoing plan by the Seychelles Dive Association and lie in a line stretching out from Corsair Reef. The deepest part of the dive is under the stern section of the outermost barge at 25 m (80 ft) and the sand scoured area under the hull is home to spiny lobsters and the poisonous striped eel catfish (*Plotosus lineatus*). These catfish live in tightly packed schools and when disturbed will all move away together until they find another section of the hull to hide under. There is another small group to be found at the bows of the barge

The spotted moray (Gymnothorax tesselata) *can be found in the area where the Corsair Reef meets the sand plane.*

The hingeback shrimp (Rhinchocinetes rugulosus) *is seen inside the barges, standing at the entrance to its cleaning station. Here you can see a juvenile on the head of the adult.*

closest to the reef. Both barges are connected by rope and then onto the reef, so it is impossible to get lost on this dive.

The barges are open and sit upright on the seabed; the sides and other areas of the superstructure are now well encrusted in all manner of soft and hard corals and sponges. Schools of glassfish inhabit the lower wreck, and the interiors of both wrecks have moray eels and lionfish (*Pterois volitans*). Pygmy pufferfish are common (*Canthogaster valentini*) as well as the hingeback shrimp (*Rhynchocinetes rugulosus*).

Continuing closer into shore you will come upon Corsair Reef, which rises steeply to only 6 m (20 ft) in the shallowest area. This reef is regularly patrolled by white-tipped reef sharks and, depending on the time of day that you dive this lovely reef, you may be lucky. There are good hard and soft coral growths with parrotfish, grouper, anemones and clownfish, and many other varieties of reef fish including the tiny longnosed filefish (*Oxymonacanthus longirostrus*) and the blotched lizardfish (*Synodus jaculum*). This is an excellent dive site, particularly as a night dive, and should not be missed, even although the visibility can be "temperamental."

Expertise Required:	Advanced
Location:	Due west from Twin Barges (Dive Site No. 10)
Typical Depth:	27 m (90 ft)
Typical Current Conditions:	Slight to Moderate
Access:	By dive boat only

The *Auberge* was sunk deliberately in 1989 onto a flat, slightly sloping sandy seabed. It now forms an excellent artificial reef, home to countless species of marine life. The wreck rolled onto its starboard side, and it is not recommended to dive down and enter the wreck due to the depth and possibility of entanglement in sections of the interior. The old tires used as mooring protection still dangle from the ship now encrusted in corals and sponges. The water column always has small numbers of batfish, and there is always a good chance to see hunting packs of tuna and bonito as they swarm over the wreck, hunting for small fish.

This diver is photographing the marine life along the hull of the Auberge *wreck.*

Expertise Required: Novice
Location: Travel west beyond Bel Ombre
Typical Depth Range: Surface to 12 m (0–40 ft)
Typical Current Conditions: Slight
Access: By dive boat only

Danzille is another shallow water dive where an outfall of granite boulders projects from the shore and forms a series of caves, archways, and overhangs, each with their own variety of life and photographic opportunity. This is a favored site for snorkeling from the dive boat along the granite edge of the shoreline where the boulders tumbled into the ocean. There are lovely pink sea fans and golden cup corals (*Tubastrea aurea*) all over the underhangs, where it is also common to see octopus. Spiny lobsters are also found in the caves and the numerous swim-throughs are a delight, but care should be taken when there is oceanic surge because there may be a good chance of being pushed into the coral encrusted rocks.

The long-spined sea urchin is common around the rocky ledges and should be avoided. The shallower areas of lower boulders also have large numbers of anemones and skunk anemonefish (*Amphiprion akallopisos*). Scorpionfish also lurk in the shadows and there is a small group of hatchetfish (*Pempheris vanicolensis*) under the larger of the boulders. In the water column it is common to see silver batfish (*Monodactylus argenteus*), as well as various species of fusilier that sweep past the reef.

The cowfish (Lactoria fornasini) *is a comical reef fish that makes an excellent photographic subject.*

Expertise Required:	Novice
Location:	West of Danzille, to the next group of granite boulders that break the surface close to the shore
Typical Depth Range:	Surface to 12 m (0–40 ft)
Typical Current Conditions:	Slight, but subject to surge
Access:	By dive boat only

This is one of my favorite sites. These huge granite blocks have a unique white gorgonian and what can only be described as "fields" of huge plate anemones each with their symbiotic partners the skunk clownfish. There are in fact three species of clownfish to be found at this location, each favoring their own particular species of anemone. Between the two largest boulders, the canyon narrows and is blocked by a tumble of huge granite blocks, which you can swim under with care. Golden cup corals and colorful bryozoans are also found in these shady areas, as well as spiny lobster and various species of shrimp.

This is a popular night diving location and well known for the abundance of invertebrates that can always be found, including several flatworms and nudibranchs or sea slugs. The spotted snake eel (*Myrichthys maculosus*)—actually a member of the conger eel family—is an active feeder around these rocks at night and hides under the sand during the daylight hours. Stingrays are common on the sandy area, as well as shrimps and gobies. The coral rubble also has brittle starfish and large pincushion sea urchins, and sea cucumbers.

Hatchetfish (Pempheris oualensis) *form small protective schools underneath the granite overhangs, preferring the shaded areas of the reef.*

Expertise Required: Intermediate
Location: The point at the eastern entrance to Baie Ternay Marine National Park (Dive Site No. 15)
Typical Depth Range: Surface to 15 m (0–50 ft)
Typical Current Conditions: Slight to moderate, stronger on the corner
Access: By dive boat only

Also known as Ray's Point or Carley's Point, Baie Ternay Point is another favorite dive, where several moray eels can be found as well as the rare black fire lionfish (*Pterois antennata*). In fact there are at least four species of lionfish to be found in Seychelles' waters. Nudibranchs are also common here and large schools of gillraker mackerel (*Rastrelliger kanagurta*) can be seen breaking the surface as they scoop up the plankton and herald the coming of manta rays and whale sharks. They are always found in association with schools of small barracudas and jacks.

The granite boulders are well encrusted with hard and soft coral growths where juvenile fish seek shelter from various predators. The sweetlips family and in particular the Oriental sweetlips (*Plectorhinchus orientalis*), which is yellow with blue/black horizontal lines, as adults are completely different from juveniles, which are brown with creamy vertical stripes and wriggle constantly under the coral heads. Moray eels are common and there are always large groupers, rays, and turtles to be seen.

The whale shark is a common visitor in the winter months, particularly November when the SUBIOS film festival is held.

Expertise Required: Novice
Location: Baie Ternay Marine National Park
Typical Depth Range: 6–25 m (20–80 ft)
Typical Current Conditions: None
Access: Can be done from the shore or by dive boat

Baie Ternay is an excellent location for snorkeling among the shallow coral heads that form a natural fringing reef around the inner shores. At only 6 m deep (20 ft) there are large numbers of different hard corals and sea fans. Moray eels are very common and are seen on every dive. Anemones and clownfish are everywhere in the shallows among small schools of wrasse and parrotfish. The wrasse family are incredibly diverse and many can only be identified after you have photographed them. Anthias goldfish (*Pseudoanthias squamipinnis*)—the same species as found in the Red Sea—is also common here.

Along the edge of the reef where the sand patch begins, there are patches of turtle grass where numerous molluscs and starfish can be found. It is here that you will encounter turtles, rays, and pelagic jacks. The bay is sheltered for most of the year and with very little commercial development, the reef remains in a pristine condition.

The starfish Protoreaster nodosus can be found on the sand plane next to the fringing coral reef on the inside of Baie Ternay Marine Park; it often has a symbiotic shrimp living on it.

Expertise Required:	Intermediate
Location:	The western point from Baie Ternay Marine National Park
Typical Depth Range:	6–30 m (20–100 ft)
Typical Current Conditions:	Moderate to strong and subject to surge
Access:	By dive boat only

This is another one of those dives onto a series of huge coral boulders with a light covering of encrusting soft and hard corals. These are simply massive blocks of granite and are quite dramatic as you approach them through the regular small groups of batfish. The boulders have also created numerous swim-throughs, which are well covered with shade-loving creatures such as small invertebrates and molluscs. Lobster are always present alongside coral grouper and lionfish. Although small creatures are all over, this is a great wide-angle photography location, but care should be taken with the time at depth, as it can be prohibitive.

The huge coral encrusted boulders litter the sandy seabed and due to the clarity of the water, it is sometimes difficult to realize that some are in 30 m (100 ft) depth; time at this depth should be closely monitored to avoid lengthy decompression stops on the way to the surface. Remember to Plan Your Dive and Dive Your Plan.

This coral crab has made its home among the low encrusting corals at the Lighthouse. Timid during the day, they are active predators at night.

Expertise Required: Intermediate
Location: South of Conception Island on the
                               inshore side of the point
Typical Depth Range: Surface to 18 m (0–60 ft)
Typical Current Conditions: Slight to moderate
Access: By dive boat only

Conception is usually done as the second dive on the way back to Beau Vallon Bay after diving Trois Banc (Dive Site No. 18). This steeply sloping granite wall is covered in a light blue soft coral amid numerous small hard corals. All of the surface area is smothered in marine life and the species of fish are prolific. Much of the hard stoney corals have teeth marks from parrotfish, which are quite voracious in this area. Wrasse are common and you should be able to watch other fish lining up to be cleaned at the various cleaning stations, where small cleaner wrasse will pick parasites and decay from any fish that requires this important reef service.

This is one of the locations where the Spanish dancer nudibranch (*Hexabranchus sanguineus*) can be found grazing on algae during the day. Normally a nocturnal species, they have a symbiotic shrimp that lives among the folds of skin. On the sandy seabed amid the coral rubble there are numerous small sea fans and fan worms.

This delicate looking "rose" is actually the egg mass of the Spanish dancer nudibranch, which lays hundreds of thousands of eggs. Considered rare in many areas of the world, the Spanish dancer (Hexabranchus sanguineus), *is common in the Seychelles, moving through the water column by body undulations.*

Expertise Required:	Advanced
Location:	Midway between Conception Island in the north and Point Lazare in the south
Typical Depth Range:	Beyond 25 m (80 ft)
Typical Current Conditions:	Moderate and subject to oceanic surge
Access:	By dive boat only

It takes around 45 minutes to motor from Beau Vallon Bay to Trois Banc, and once or twice we have been caught in tropical rain storms that completely obliterated our sight of land for a short time, preventing us from seeing the transit points for the submerged rocks until the storm passed. Generally subject to oceanic surge due to its exposed position, Trois Banc is one of the better dives for the more experienced diver.

These are a series of huge granite blocks that rise about 10 m from the seabed (33 ft). These blocks are covered in soft and hard corals as well as vast sections of fire coral. (Fire coral [*Millepora sp.*] is not a true coral, but actually a member of the hydroid family). Large schools of batfish immediately approach as you descend to the seabed. Schools of small wrasse are common as well as fusiliers, parrotfish, and small groups of eagle rays (*Aetobatus narinari*). Moray eels are always present as well as lobster and numerous species of shrimp and sea urchins. Grouper also grow to quite large sizes around these granitic blocks, because there is no commercial fishing in this region. Trois Banc is an excellent dive site and well worth the extra travel time.

Typical of dives in the open waters of the Seychelles, batfish are a common companion.

Expertise Required:	Novice
Location:	West of Grand Anse and south of Port Launay Marine National Park
Typical Depth Range:	Surface to 12 m (0–40 ft)
Typical Current Conditions:	Slight to moderate on the exposed corners
Access:	By dive boat only

This is a lovely vegetated island off the west coast, primarily of granite, but with lush growth topped by tropical palms. The shoreline slopes downwards on the outer edges to more than 12 m (40 ft) and is made up of large overlapping granite blocks covered in soft and hard corals, giant anemones, and pink sea fans. Again, this appears to be a favorite area for finding juvenile fish and invertebrates. Being so close to the Port Launay Marine National Park, there is an obvious overspill of marine life species and the protection offered by Isle Therese attracts many different forms of marine life.

There are numerous varieties of angelfish and butterflyfish, as well as filefish, sweetlips, snapper, and grouper. Members of the wrasse family are the most common, and they can be found in their multitude all over the coral encrusted blocks and sandy rubble seabed.

Darkband fusiliers (Pterocaesio tile) *are sift hunters, forever moving around the offshore islands and coral reefs.*

Expertise Required:	Intermediate
Location:	West of the Dauban river south of Grand Anse
Typical Depth Range:	20 m (66 ft)
Typical Current Conditions:	Moderate to strong
Access:	By dive boat only

Small rounded granite boulders surround some simply massive formations that have created a small island close to shore. Although the only access is by boat, the snorkeling around these granite outcrops is very interesting indeed. Parrotfish and wrasse abound in the shallows and skunk anemonefish are common all around the shoreline. As you travel farther underwater, past a rim of fire coral and hard Acropora corals, there is a large area of leather corals and small encrusting soft corals. It is here that the largest number of invertebrates can be found. Spiny sea urchins are common, and if you look closely, you should be able to see a commensal shrimp among the spines. The pincushion starfish also has a species of shrimp that lives on the outside of the large, leathery shell.

The sand and coral rubble seabed is home to many molluscs, gobies, and tiny wrasse. Sea cucumbers are common and the whole area appears to be alive with fish. The area can be subject to oceanic swells from the west, and Iles aux Vaches will only be visited when the conditions are perfect. This whole area is similar to Trois Bancs (Dive Site No. 18), but different in that there is more likelihood of seeing sharks and turtles on this dive.

A diver approaches a pair of pincushion sea urchins (Cultica novaeguineae). *These are fairly common on all of the granite outcroppings.*

Expertise Required:	Intermediate
Location:	North of Pointe Lazare, west of Anse a la Mouche
Typical Depth Range:	Surface–15 m (0–50 ft)
Typical Current Conditions:	Slight to moderate
Access:	By dive boat only

This little rocky islet is very reminiscent of L'Ilot west of North Point (Dive Site No. 4). Vertical and near vertical huge granite boulders form a mini-wall most of the way around the island, creating areas covered in *Dendrophyllia,* which typically is small clusters of single coral polyps, but in this case has created huge expanses of vivid color that is absolutely incredible during a night dive.

Moray eels are always present and are generally surrounded by their attendant cleaner shrimp (*Stenopus hispidus* and *Rhynchocinetes rugulosa*), which can be found in large numbers. Cowrie shells are common as well as murex and the false cowrie (*Ovula ovum*), which has a pure white shell and jet black mantle with tiny gold spots. The area is filled with fish, and there are more than enough photographic subjects here to bring you back time after time.

The false cowrie (Ovula ovum) is commonly found feeding on soft and leather corals that grow in profusion all over the granite islands.

Expertise Required:	Intermediate
Location:	Southwest of Takamaka
Typical Depth Range:	Surface–12 m (0–40 ft)
Typical Current Conditions:	Moderate
Access:	By dive boat only

   This is another popular and very interesting series of granitic boulders off the southwest of Mahé. The moderate current that passes around the southwestern corner of the island and through these rocks accounts for some surprising marine life discoveries. White and pink gorgonian sea fans seem to crowd the narrow gullies that have formed under the tumbled blocks of granite. Glassy sweepers, coral trout, and lobsters are always present and again, large numbers of anemones and their symbiotic partners, the clownfish, are found; in fact, two species are found close to each other. Around the folds of these anemones, you should also be able to find the spotted anemone crab (*Neopetrolisthes maculatus*) and the spotted cleaner shrimp (*Periclemenes brevicarpalis*). Common starfish include several species of *Linkia* as well as the much smaller and brightly colored *Fromia monilis*.

Linkia starfish come in various colors, from brilliant yellow to blue to black with red stripes; they grow up to half a meter long (20 inches).

Expertise Required:	Novice
Location:	Due east of Anse Aux Pins, south of the airport
Typical Depth Range:	3–9 m (10–30 ft)
Typical Current Conditions:	Slight
Access:	By dive boat only

The outer edge of this barrier reef is well offshore and although it can be reached by snorkeling, it is rather far. However, the snorkeling in the sheltered lagoon is excellent with many small coral heads primarily of staghorn coral (*Acropora robusta* and *Acropora verweberi*). Around these are schools of chromis that dart among the coral heads for protection when you approach them. On the sandy floor of the lagoon are small mushroom corals (*Fungia fungites*), which are individual polyps not attached to other corals. Numerous molluscs also inhabit this area.

The outward edge of this barrier reef is best reached by the local dive boats, which will remain on station above you as you cruise along the steeply sloping mini-wall. Although the reef can be affected by an unseasonal surge, overall it is an excellent dive. Leather corals and small clumps of stony corals predominate. Anemones are common and the reef is teeming with fish life including lionfish, scorpionfish, parrotfish, and wrasse. On the coral rubble and sand seabed you will encounter small rays as well as the ubiquitous gobies and shrimp in their sand burrows.

Acropora *corals stretch out on this long barrier reef on the east coast.*

Expertise Required:	Novice
Location:	East of Victoria and encompasses Cerf Island, Round Island, St. Anne, Moyenne, Long Island, and Beacon Rock
Typical Depth Range:	Surface–15 m (0–50 ft)
Typical Current Conditions:	Slight
Access:	By dive boat only

This national marine nature reserve is just a short distance from Victoria harbor and is a favorite location for glass-bottomed boats and snorkelers around the shallower coral gardens. This is one of the first views that you get of Seychelles waters as you approach the runway, which is just south of the marine reserve. (So, for the best view, ask for a window seat on the right hand side of the airplane). From the air, the sea looks as if it is made of multi-colored layers of blue and turquoise pigmentation and is very picturesque.

Underwater, the views are just as good. Visibility can be reduced in the shallower sandy areas, but most of the diving takes place around the Beacon Rock area where the seabed is covered in acropora corals and anemones. It was here that I saw my first trumpet triton shell (*Charonia tritonis*), the natural enemy of the crown of thorns starfish, which also occurs on these coral reefs, but thankfully in very small numbers. Triton shells have also been known to eat pincushion starfish. There is an above-average chance of seeing large jacks, tuna, turtles, and rays around the outer granite outcrops. This area offers excellent diving and is a favored location during the winter months of December through March.

The green turtle (Chelonia mydas) *is much more common in recent years now that it is completely protected.*

4

Praslin and La Digue Dive Sites

Praslin is only 35 minutes flying time northeast of the airport on Mahé. The island-hopping service run by Air Seychelles fills a much needed service between the outer islands also under Seychelles control. Small airstrips are located on Assumption, Astove, Desroches, North Island at Farquar, Desnoeufs, D'arros, Bird Island, Frégate, Denis and Coetivy.

Praslin is like stepping back in time. There is a much more relaxed atmosphere to the whole island, and visitors should not just limit themselves to diving. The Vallée de Mai is an outstanding national nature reserve of great importance and has many different specimens of ancient flora and fauna, many found nowhere else in the world. Hire (rental) cars are available from the small airport, but most hotels will arrange for your transfer to and from the airport.

Dive Site Ratings	Novice	Intermediate	Advanced
25 Red Point	x	x	x
26 Coral Gardens	x	x	x
27 Booby Island		x	x
28 Aride Bank*		x	x
29 Cousin		x	x
30 Cousine		x	x
31 East Sister Bank		x	x
32 Ave Maria Rocks*	x	x	x
33 South Felicité		x	x
34 Anse Severe*	x	x	x
35 Renomeé Rocks		x	x

*Excellent snorkeling

Praslin & La Digue

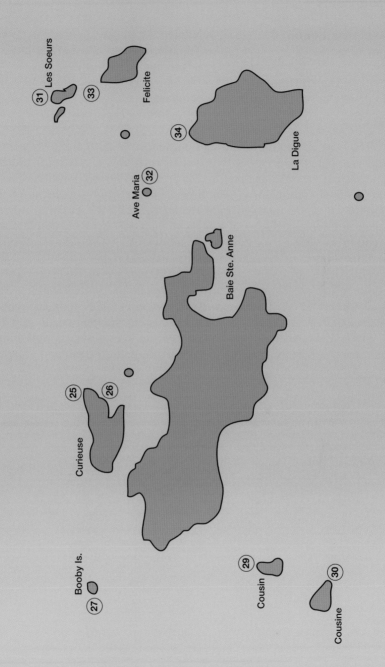

Les Soeurs

㉛

㉝

Felicite

㉞ La Digue

㉟

㉜ Ave Maria

Baie Ste. Anne

㉕ ㉖

Curieuse

Booby Is.

㉗

㉙ Cousin

㉚ Cousine

Aride

㉘

Expertise Required:	Novice
Location:	The northeastern point of Curieuse Island, north of Praslin
Typical Depth Range:	10–14 m (33–45 ft)
Typical Current Conditions:	Moderate
Access:	By dive boat only

Red Point is best dived during optimum conditions from March to May and October to December, when the prevailing winds offer protection. The sea can be quite choppy in this area, and surge conditions can make entry and exit from a dive boat difficult. The terrain is made up of granite boulders that are tumbled together on the seafloor, creating interesting swim-throughs, gullies, and mini-wall canyons. Stingrays are a common sighting as well as the fimbriated moray eel (*Gymnothorax fimbriatus*) and the spotted snake eel (*Myrichthys maculosus*).

This site is also well known for its abundance of angelfish. The most common are the Koran angelfish (*Pomacanthus semicirculatus*) and the emperor angelfish (*Pomacanthus imperator*). The monacle hawkfish (*Paracirrhites arcatus*) can be seen resting on the small growths of staghorn coral. Anemones and clownfish are in evidence as well as numerous snapper, parrotfish, wrasse, damselfish, butterflyfish, and groupers.

Scorpionfish can be found on most dives and normally have superb camouflage, unlike this bright pink specimen.

Expertise Required:	Novice
Location:	In the sheltered bay of Curieuse before Red Point
Typical Depth Range:	10–14 m (33–45 ft)
Typical Current Conditions:	Slight
Access:	By dive boat only

Well named, this is an area of soft and hard coral growth similar to the shallow areas of the Baie Ternay Marine National Park (Dive Site No. 15). Large tuna and amberjacks sweep into this bay in search of easy pickings. There are large numbers of angelfish, butterflyfish, parrotfish, and wrasse. Barracuda are seen in small hunting packs and all of the larger coral heads have their antendant schools of chromis. Sergeant majors are accustomed to divers and will follow you around, as do the large batfish (*Platax orbicularis*).

The Coral Gardens Bay is subject to weather variations that can reduce visibility, and it is always better to check in advance to see if the conditions are favorable. When I first dived in this location, there was torrential rain and the visibility had dropped to around 5 m (15 ft). However, this phenomenon is purely seasonal and for the greater part of the time, the visibility is excellent above and below the waves.

This tiny relative of the scorpionfish—often called the pygmy scorpionfish (Sebastapistes cyanostigma)—is a real treat to find hiding deep within the protection of coral heads.

Expertise Required:	Intermediate
Location:	Midway between Praslin and Aride
Typical Depth Range:	12–25 m (40–80 ft)
Typical Current Conditions:	Moderate
Access:	By dive boat only

This dive site, sometimes known as Booby Rock, is also only dived when the weather conditions are perfect and then only generally from March to May and October to December. Strong tidal streams and oceanic swell can result in an uncomfortable ride to and from the dive site, but the underwater terrain and marine life is well worth the effort. Booby Island is known as one of the feeding areas for whale sharks and manta rays, November and May being the best months to view these ocean wanderers. Turtle, large tuna, rays, and sharks are often seen, and the large granite and coral outcroppings are home to myriad marine creatures. Schools of dolphins often accompany the dive boat between the dive sites.

At the bottom of the coral encrusted granite boulders can be found large overhangs where lobster and moray eels are always found. Large groupers inhabit the shaded areas alongside lionfish, waiting to pick off individuals from the schools of glassy sweepers that are all around. This is a very good dive site.

The polyps of golden cup corals remain closed during daylight hours and can be found on the lower slopes of granite boulders amid bright red sponges.

Expertise Required:	Intermediate
Location:	North west of Praslin and off the west end of Aride
Typical Depth Range:	6–18 m (20–60 ft)
Typical Current Conditions:	Moderate
Access:	By dive boat only

The western shores of Aride slope out in a tumble of granite boulders that provide excellent snorkeling around this world-renowned bird sanctuary. The western shores fall away much more steeply and the granite cliff forms miniwalls with extensive growths of soft and hard corals and small sea fans in the crevices. Fire coral is abundant, but there are huge numbers of fish not normally found around the commoner dive sites on the main island of Mahé or Praslin.

Butterflyfish species include bannerfish (*Heniochus intermedius*) and Meyer's butterflyfish (*Chaetodon meyeri*). Royal angelfish (*Pygoplites diacanthus*) and threespot angelfish (*Apolemichthys trimaculatus*) are also present, as are grunts, snappers and sweetlips. More uncommon crustaceans include the tiny spider crab of the *Xenocarcinus* family, which lives on the seafans and is rarely spotted during daylight hours.

Pink gorgonian seafans are very much a feature of diving around the main Seychelles group of islands; all are found in areas of current.

63

Expertise Required:	Intermediate
Location:	3 km (2 mi) southeast of Praslin, to the north shore of the island
Typical Depth Range:	10–18 m (33–60 ft)
Typical Current Conditions:	Moderate and subject to surge
Access:	By dive boat only

The dive site off the north shore of Cousin is known locally as Hauts Roches and is a series of granitic boulders heavily encrusted with low colonies of soft and hard corals. Being exposed to the oceanic swell, this site is best dived from May to June and September to November. On every dive you can expect to see moray eels of several species and size, and literally thousands of chromis, wrasse, parrotfish, butterflyfish, and angelfish. This is a very prolific site with much of the boulders covered in the light blue leather coral (*Sarcophyton glaucum*) and *Acropora* species.

As in most of these offshore locations, due to the limited diving done on them, there is a very high probability of seeing spotted eagle rays, stingrays, white-tipped reef sharks, and nurse sharks. Turtles are common as are other large pelagics such as dog-toothed tuna and jacks.

Cousin is owned by the Royal Society for Nature Conservation and is administered by the International Council of Bird Preservation. Visitors are limited to 20 and then only on three days each week.

Angelfish are always a delight to find and photograph, many of which will pose quite readily; this is the Koran angelfish (Pomacanthus semicirculatus).

Expertise Required: Intermediate
Location: 1½ km (1 mi) southeast of Cousin Island
                             to the dive site off the southeastern
                             point of the island
Typical Depth Range: 14–18 m (45–60 ft)
Typical Current Conditions: Moderate and subject to surge
Access: By dive boat only

This southern area off the island of Cousine is also well known for spotting whale sharks and manta rays. These have been seen frequently by the local Air Seychelles island-hopping service and the tourism helicopter, which always radio ahead to the local dive centers to give the position of these gentle giants.

This site is best dived from May to June and September to November when the winds are from the northeast, providing the maximum shelter from Praslin Island. The dive is onto a series of submerged granite boulders that have formed numerous gullies and swim-throughs, which are smothered in golden cup coral (*Tubastrea aurea*), bright yellow and orange shade-loving sponges, and on the upwards slopes, fire coral and spiny sea urchins. In the more current-swept areas, there are large aggregations of anemones with clownfish and damselfish vying for the photographer's attention. Groupers lurk in the shadows, and overall, the underwater view is very scenic with above average visibility.

Radianthus ritteri is one of the smaller anemones that occur in these waters, and is distinctive by the white tips of its tentacles.

Expertise Required:	Intermediate
Location:	To the north of the eastern island called Grande Soeur; dive off the northern shelf where the granite boulders are prominent
Typical Depth Range:	12–20 m (40–66 ft)
Typical Current Conditions:	Moderate to strong
Access:	By dive boat only

The Twin Sisters as they are known (Petite Soeur and Grande Soeur) are a popular dive location and are dived from February to November. Typically granite in formation, the boulders are enormous and an oasis of life. Large hard corals extend outward amid patchy, but brilliantly colored soft corals. White-tipped reef sharks (*Triaenodon obesus*) are commonly found resting under the granite outcrops, as are nurse sharks (*Nebrius ferrugineus*). The large black-spotted ribbontail stingray (*Taeniura melanospilos*) is also noted as well as numerous other interesting fish species.

Pufferfish are common here, and there are at least six distinct species from the smallest—Valentine's sharpnosed puffer (*Canthigaster valentini*)—to the largest—the yellowspotted burrfish (*Chilomycterus spilostylus*). **Note:** Please do not handle the larger spiny globefish or burrfish to make them inflate. This causes distress to the fish and the rough handling can remove the protective mucus from the outer skin of the fish, which can result in infection and even death of the fish, if handled enough times.

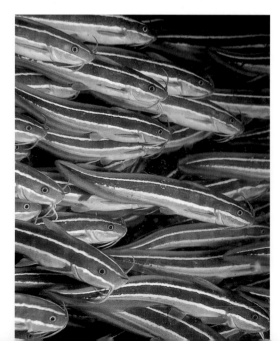

Striped eel-catfish (Plotosus lineatus) *can be found in large groups when they are juveniles, moving in unison along the reef as they search for small fish and crustaceans as food.*

Expertise Required:	Novice
Location:	Midway between Felicité and Praslin
Typical Depth Range:	8–20 m (27–66 ft)
Typical Current Conditions:	Moderate, but can be oceanic surge
Access:	By dive boat only

Ave Maria Rocks can only be dived when conditions are perfect, from March to May and October to December. This offshore granite outcrop seems to channel the plankton as it sweeps in from the Indian Ocean, bringing with it mackerel, manta rays and whale sharks. This is a superb site for diving with these creatures, but luck has to be with you. November is the best month for whale sharks.

The site is very reminiscent of Brissaire Rocks off Mahé (Dive Site No. 2) and can be subject to swell and surge conditions, subsequently there are large areas of fire coral, and low encrusting hard and soft corals. Large numbers of parrotfish and wrasse move among the coral branches, and sweetlips and groupers hold their position in the numerous cleaning stations that dot the edges of the coral-encrusted boulders.

Schools of glassfish congregate in localized areas, moving as one, always just out of one's reach.

Expertise Required: Intermediate
Location: Granite boulders in the channel south of
                                 Felicité Island to the west of Praslin
Typical Depth Range: 10–16 m (33–52 ft)
Typical Current Conditions: Moderate to strong and surge conditions
Access: By dive boat only

The southern point of Felicité is another superb section of granite boulders covered in coral growth. This simply is a superb dive site, with numerous shoals and reefs that break the surface and then plummet down in a series of miniwalls. There can be oceanic surge and reduced visibility occasionally, but the main currents flow in and around Praslin and her islets along this rugged channel. Again, when the seasonal plankton bloom occurs in the April/May and October/November periods, you will encounter whale sharks and manta rays, marlin, and tuna. The whole area is filled with marine life from the tiniest of shrimp to the largest of wrasse, the humphead or Napoleon wrasse (*Cheilinus undulatus*).

Cleaning stations are very noticeable in this area, where tiny shrimp and members of the wrasse family clean parasites and decay from all those who wish it, including us divers! See page 81 for more information on cleaning stations.

This beautiful species of tube worm (Sabellastartia magnifica) *is just one of the many different types of animals that make up the complex ecosystem of the reefs.*

Expertise Required:	Intermediate
Location:	Off the northern tip of La Digue Island
Typical Depth Range:	6–16 m (20–52 ft)
Typical Current Conditions:	Slight to moderate
Access:	By dive boat only

This dive is also only done seasonally and then only when wind and water conditions are perfect. The headland off the north point of La Digue is subject to oceanic swell, and surge conditions will exist, making for an uncomfortable boat ride. When conditions are best, from March to May and October to December, then there appears to be an above average representation of marine life.

Large granite boulders are encrusted in fire coral, hard and soft corals, sea anemones, hydroids, and tiny sea squirts. There are at least three species of tubeworms to be found here—*Spirobranchus giganteus,* which is found in all of the world's tropical oceans; a more delicate relative called *Protula magnifica;* and a much larger specimen, which is a member of the *Sabellidae* family. The abundance of tubeworms and expanses of low sea fans, all indicate a large concentration of planktonic particles to feed these tiny animals.

Scorpionfish are quite common, as are octopus and reef squid. Sea urchins and cucumbers can be found everywhere and fish life includes Bengal snapper (*Lutjanus bengalensis*) Oriental sweetlips (*Plectorhinchus orientalis*) and common bigeye (*Priacanthus hamrur*). When conditions are perfect and no tide running, this is also an excellent snorkeling site, but care must be taken.

The longnoxed hawkfish (Oxycirrhitus typus) *is always a joy to find hiding among the branches of gorgonian fan corals.*

Expertise Required:	Intermediate
Location:	3 km (2 mi) south of La Digue
Typical Depth Range:	10–30 m (33–100 ft)
Typical Current Conditions:	Moderate to strong
Access:	By dive boat only

These offshore granite rocks have formed small islets that are a natural attraction for all manner of marine life. Available to dive from September to May, although they can be rather exposed, there are always sheltered sections to allow you safe diving. Moray eels are quite common and several species are seen regularly. All have attendant, brightly colored cleaner shrimp.

Lionfish are common as well as butterflyfish, angelfish, parrotfish, and wrasse. Longnose filefish (*Oxymonacanthus longirostris*) can be seen around *Acropora* coral and the rare clown triggerfish (*Balistoides conspicillum*) is not so rare around these offshore boulders. Miniwalls are covered in soft corals and golden cup coral, where murex shells blend in with the same coloration. Schools of bigmouth mackerel (*Rastrelliger kanagurta*) occur near the reef and in the upper water column where they filter plankton. It is quite interesting to watch as all of the fish drop their lower jaws at the same time and sweep through the water.

It is true to say that the farther offshore that you travel around the Seychelles, the more interesting the marine life is. These granite boulders and islets are only rarely dived, but are highly recommended, whenever you get the chance.

The coral grouper (Cephalopholis miniata) *is one of the most comon groupers in the Indian and Pacific Oceans and can be seen on almost every dive in the Seychelles.*

Divers pass some of the abundant stands of black coral and attendant schools of tiny fish that characterize many of Seychelles' offshore dives. ▶

5

Marine Life of the Seychelles

The Family Groups

Most types of marine life are relatively unknown to the average reader without specific knowledge of marine biology, so I will first give a summary of the groups of plants and animals to be found around the Seychelles coast and islands.

The *Porifera* or sponges are animals of so simple a structure that they are more like an aggregation or colony of protozoans. In Seychelles waters, they are small, encrusting, brightly colored and found in shaded areas. They are always attached to rocks and corals.

The *Coelenterata* include many relatively simple animals and can be divided into two major groups—those attached like the anemones and those free swimming like the jellyfish. Most of the larger anemones in the Seychelles have symbiotic relationships with several other species including shrimps, crabs, and anemonefish, or clownfish. Many of the attached family group members are not solitary like the anemones, but consist of many united individuals like the stinging hydroid (*Lytocarpus philippinus*). Allied more closely to the anemones are the soft corals, or *Alcyonarians,* which consist of many individuals sharing a common skeleton of a horny substance; and the true corals, *Scleractina,* which have massive calcareous skeletons.

The *Tunicata* are exclusively marine and comprise many animals of different appearances. This group includes the sea squirts and ascidians, some of the smallest of which are the species of *Didemnum,* which are tiny and come in many different colors.

The *Turbellaria,* or flatworms, are seldom more than 2.5 cm long, flat, very colorful and sometimes parasitic, they are able to swim freely in the water column by muscular undulations of their bodies. The *Nemertea* are soft-bodied worms that have a proboscis and are without the division of the body into transverse segments. The *Polychaeta* are perhaps the most common and include tubeworms such as the Christmas tree worm (*Spirobranchus giganteus*). Many wander freely (errant worms) and others (sedentary worms) always live in tubes of lime, sand or parchment-like material, which they make themselves and enlarge as they grow. Many of the types of worms have little in common with one another except their general shape.

The *Echinodermata* is a very diverse group and includes the starfish and sea urchin. They are mostly slow moving, locomotion being provided by the peculiar tube feet through a "hydraulics" network of water supplied by canals throughout the body. There are five distinct groups: the starfish, *Asteroidea;* the brittlestars, *Ophiuroidea;* the sea urchins, *Echinoidea;* the sea cucumbers, *Holothuroidea;* and finally the feather stars and sea lilies, *Crinoidea.*

The *Arthropoda* include the largest number of species of any group in the animal kingdom. Like the annelid worms, they have segmented bodies, but have jointed limbs attached, which give the group their name. Of the four great divisions, three—insect, spider and centipede classes—are found almost exclusively on land, and the fourth, *Crustacea,* is almost entirely marine. It is a very broad group that includes water fleas, barnacles, sand hoppers, shrimps, prawns, lobsters, hermit crabs, and many species of true crabs.

The *Mollusca* is another group of considerable variety and includes nudibranchs, chitons, and octopus. The *Gastropoda* or univalved shellfish such as limpets, periwinkles, and snails usually have a shell of one piece and live mostly on the shore or sea bottom, but a few with greatly reduced shells swim near the surface. *Bivalvia,* the bivalve molluscs, have a shell composed of more or less equal halves; another great division is the highly organized *Cephalopoda,* which includes squid, octopus, and cuttlefish, distinguished by their eight or ten tentacles or arms. A similar group are the *Brachiapoda,* often mistaken for molluscs.

Fish are divided into two principal groups, the *Elasmobranchs,* which include dogfish, sharks, and skate, and have a relatively soft cartilaginous skeleton with the gill openings separate; and *Teleosts,* or bony fish, which have hard boney skeletons, and their gill openings are covered by flaps.

Cetacea are the air breathers, and include whales, dolphins, and porpoises. They usually live on or near the surface, but are capable of diving to considerable depth, though they are always compelled to return to the surface for air.

The Coral Reefs of the Seychelles

As mentioned, the main group of the Seychelles Islands are the granite tips of a submarine plateau. The islands are volcanic in origin and covered with dense subtropical and tropical vegetation. During the monsoon season, the islands' rivers become swollen and the subsequent rain-water runoff can affect the surrounding area and reduce the water visibility. This also accounts for some of the corals being low and encrusting, because they do not like fresh water or colder temperatures. Due to the Seychelles having primarily a fringing reef, which is only a step away, much of the diving is either very close to the shore or on the offshore granite boulders that are so synonymous with Seychelles diving. By far the greatest proportion of diving is from dive boats. There is shore diving in several locations and you can snorkel just about everywhere. Much of the coastline lies within the protection of a fringing reef, and this sheltered lagoon environment is not only a safe haven for swimming and snorkeling, it is also the major breeding area for many species of fish and invertibrates.

The sublittoral region can be divided into several different areas or habitats. Directly from the shore you will encounter a *fringing reef.* In most cases this is fairly flat and sandy on the top due to the constant battering it has received over the centuries by tide, weather, and man. You'll also encounter the occasional knob of hard coral such as *Acropora* sp. In the open sand areas you will generally find turtle grass. The sand areas drop down to an outer fringing reef on the other side of the lagoon or form a much larger *barrier reef* consisting of staghorn and brain corals. Barrier reefs grow parallel to the coastline, and the best example is off Anse Aux Pins, south of the International Airport.

Beyond this shallower drop you will find a steeply inclined *sand stage* interspaced with low encrusting clumps of hard and soft coral, often attached to granite boulders. Coral clumps are sometimes known as "bommies," but are generally referred to as a *patch reef* system.

The out-lying granite boulders are sometimes of such vast size that they have created *mini walls,* which are also covered in encrusting corals. The only true drop-offs in the Seychelles Islands are out on Desroches, Aldabra, etc. These inshore granite boulders are also interspaced with gullies, canyons, tunnels, and caves.

The corals themselves come in many different shapes and sizes. Remember that what you are actually seeing of the coral reef is only the outer layers. Most of the reef consists of a thin crust of living organisms building over the ancient skeletons of past coral reefs, changing in shape and structure as the environment changes around it. Soft corals are profuse, but they do not grow nearly as large as those same species to be found elsewhere in the Indo-Pacific region. The most common soft coral species are members of the *Dendronephthya,* which come in many different colors. Although classed as soft corals, because they can bend and sway in the current, they are constructed with hard calcium spicules or spikes to give them strength and can scratch the softer parts of your skin if you are not careful. The largest of the hard or stoney corals (the major reef builders) in Seychelles waters is *Porites* sp.—each individual colony can grow up to 3 m (10 ft). Other species include organ-pipe coral (*Tubipora musica*), which is quite fragile and is often washed up on the beach after an occasional storm. This coral is made up of tiny tubes—almost like bamboo—all linked together and a very dark red in color.

Brain corals such as *Platygyra daedalea* can grow up to 1 m (3 ft) across. On the more shaded areas of the boulders can be found large areas of golden cup-coral (*Tubastrea aurea*). Although the polyps are closed during the day, at night these walls are ablaze with color.

Gorgonian sea fans also come in many different varieties, and the central location of the Seychelles in the Indian Ocean allows for a higher than average representation of species to be found; although in the main group of islands around Mahé and Praslin, the most common are species of *Acabaria,* which are pinkish white in color.

Always be careful when approaching these corals, because they bend and sway in the current and it is very easy to misjudge your distance underwater and perhaps bump into them. Fan corals are also home to a vast number of invertebrates such as nudibranchs, shrimp, and filefish.

Invertebrates

About 88% of all living creatures in the sea are invertebrates, and the Seychelles, due to their central location in the Indian Ocean, just 4° south of the Equator, have a very high proportion of all the species found in these seas.

There are sponges, jellyfish, hydroids, anemones, corals, tubeworms, flatworms, segmented worms, crustaceans, molluscs, echinoderms, bryozoans, and tunicates. Their lives make up the stuff that virtually everything else depends on.

There are several species of sponge in the Seychelles, and they can be found in large numbers in the more shaded areas under the granite boulders. These include *Cliona schmidti,* which is a dark red in color, *Adocia* sp. are orange; and *Leucetta* sp. are yellow.

Jellyfish and hydroids are a closely related species. In essence, the jellyfish is a free-swimming stage of the same type of creature as the hydroid. Anemones are another relative and all are armed with stinging cells with which to paralyze their prey. The moon jellyfish (*Aurelia aurita*) is one of the few animals found in every ocean of the world. The more common hydroid you may encounter is the stinging hydroid (*Lytocarpus philippinus*). The feather-like plumes may inflict a rather nasty sting on the softer areas of your skin if you brush up against them.

The anemones of the Seychelles come in many different shapes and sizes. The giant anemone (*Stichodactylus gigantea*) is perhaps the most common and has quite long greenish tentacles. In association with this anemone, you may find other invertebrate animals such as shrimp and crab. The most vividly colored anemone found on Mahé is the magnificent anemone (*Heteractis magnifica*); the under mantle or main body of the anemone can vary from vivid red to the deepest purple. They always have clownfish living in association with them. On the sandy areas at night you may come across the burrowing anemone (*Dofleinia*).

There are several types of segmented or tubeworms around the reefs, including the magnificent featherduster worm (*Sabellastarte sancti-*

josephi) and perhaps the most beautiful of all is the Christmas tree worm (*Spirobranchus giganteus*). The Christmas tree worm is aptly named, but is only 3 cm high (1.5 in.). It comes in a multitude of colors and is more often noticed when it disappears rapidly down into its tubes in the coral when you swim close.

The banded coral shrimp (*Stenopus hispidus*) is also found in all of the tropical oceans. This is a colorful small shrimp with long pincers. It is normally the waving of the antennae that first attracts you to this creature; they are generally found in association with moray eels. The red hinge-back shrimp (*Rhynchocinetes rugulosa*) is usually spotted at night by its bright green reflective eyes, but they can be found often under shaded areas of the granite boulders which predominate the substrate. Other small shrimps include *Thor amboinensis* and *Periclemenes brevicarpalis,* which can be found on most anemones. *Periclemenes imperator* is by far the most adaptive to its environment, living on pincushion starfish, sea cucumbers, and even on the backs of Spanish dancer nudibranchs.

Slipper lobsters and spiny lobsters inhabit the reef ledges. Perhaps the most comical of all the crustaceans are the hermit crabs. The red reef hermit (*Dardanus guttatus*) can be quite wary of divers and retreat into its mobile home. *Dardanus pedunctulatus* is found in a shell covered in *Calliactis* anemones, which it uses for protection.

The Mollusc family is well represented and the range and diversity of the animals in it is vast. There are the shells of course—the conch (*Cassis cornuta* and *Lambis truncata*). The tiger cowrie (*Cyprae tigris*) is very attractive and is the largest of the cowrie shells found in the Seychelles. The false cowrie (*Ovula ovum*) is also found feeding on leathery corals; its yellow speckled black mantle folds up around the white body of the shell.

Nudibranchs or sea slugs are very attractive, and it is always a rare pleasure when you find them. They feed on a number of different animals and algae and are invariably brightly colored. The most popular of all is the Spanish dancer (*Hexabranchus sanguineus*), which is active during night dives. Look closely and you will see the brilliant red colored egg "rose" attached to a dead section of coral.

Octopus and squid are aften found prowling the Seychelles reefs at night. The squid in particular appear fascinated by divers' lights and the obvious food that these lights attract. Crinoids or featherstarfish crawl out onto the coral surface as night falls and brittlestarfish curl around the sea fans and whips. Basketstarfish extend their multi-jointed arms into the current and sea urchins vie for space amid the sponges and corals. Sea urchins, although best avoided at all times, often have other animals living among their spines and can be examined much closer if you are careful with your bouyancy.

Fish of the Seychelles

The following is a brief description of several of the more flamboyant or colorful characters on the reef. Please note that a number of species are indeed poisonous or may sting or bite. Wild animals (and fish are no exception) must be approached carefully and sympathetically. Any creature that does not move when you approach it will have some other means of defense, so PLEASE BE CAREFUL.

There are five species of rays found regularly in Seychelles waters. The manta ray (*Manta birostris*) is often accompanied by a couple of remoras or sucker-fish attached to its flanks. The remora (*Echeneis naucrates*) hitches a ride on mantas, sharks, and turtles and eats any scraps left behind by its host. The spotted eagle ray (*Aetobatus narinari*) is often found off Trois Bancs (Dive Site No. 18). This large ray has a snout somewhat like that of a pig's, and it uses it to dig and forage beneath the sand for crustaceans and molluscs. The electric or torpedo ray (*Torpedo pantheri*) is much smaller in size and grows up to a length of around 50 cm (15 in.). The rounded body has two electrical organs with which it stuns its prey. They should be treated with respect. The electrical charge is between 14–37 volts. The blue-spotted stingray (*Taeniura lymma*) is quite common on the sandy areas between the granite boulders and grows to a maximum of only 50 cm (15 in.). It is circular in shape, covered in bright blue spots, and has a strong tail with a venomous spine near the end. The largest of the stingray species, and often encountered out at Shark Bank (Dive Site No. 3) is the blackspotted ribbontail ray (*Taeniura melanospilos*).

Sharks are uncommon, but the most frequently sighted are nurse sharks (*Nebrius ferrugineus*). Distinguishable by the two barbels on the top of its lip and small mouth, it is a fairly docile creature unless disturbed. There's also the whitetipped reef shark (*Triaenodon obesus*), and if you are extremely lucky during the winter, you may get the chance to dive with the largest fish in the sea, the whale shark (*Rhincodon typus*).

Moray eels are very common around all of the Seychelles islands and there two species of conger and snake eels. The giant moray (*Gymnothorax javanicus*) is the largest of all the eels found in the Seychelles. The peppered moray (*Siderea grisea*) at only 38 cm (1 ft) long is perhaps the most common around all of the islands. They hide during the day in recesses in the reef and are active predators by night. They are quite easily approached and have the habit of opening and closing their mouth, which looks threatening, but is actually an aid to respiration. The undulate moray (*Gymnothorax undulatus*) is an aggressive (and common!) eel. Its head often protrudes from the reef. The much rarer snowflake moray (*Echidna nebulosa*) is slightly smaller with a large, dark brown to black body, irregular yellow bars and spots, yellow eyes, and a cream nose and mouth.

Snake eels have a fin which travels along the length of the back. They live under the sand during the day and are active foragers at night. The most common of the species recorded in the Seychelles during night dives is the spotted snake eel (*Myrichthys maculosus*). The garden eel (*Heteroconger hassi*) lives in vertical burrows in the softer sand areas and quite often large numbers of them can be seen swaying gently in the current, picking off plankton as it drifts past. They are extremely shy and withdraw into their burrows long before you reach them for a closer look! Striped eel catfish (*Plotosus lineatus*) are commonly found in large groups around the Twin Barges wrecks (Dive Site No. 10).

The grouper family comprise some 16 species. One of the most common and colorful groupers is the jewel grouper (*Cephalopholis miniata*), which is rather small, only growing to 50 cm (15 in.). The largest of the family group is the potato cod (*Epinephelus tukula*), which can grow up to 2 m (7 ft) long. Sadly, these are now rare due to predation by man over the centuries. One of the most common of the smaller groupers is the blacktipped grouper (*Epinephelus fasciatus*). This amusing fish, which can grow to 40 cm (16 in.), appears to be always standing guard on a coral head waiting for a tasty morsel to swim by. They come in various color variations from a dark reddish-brown to a striped variety.

The redbanded hawkfish (*Cirrhtops fasciatus*) can be found dotted around the soft and hard coral heads. The most colorful of the species is the longnosed hawkfish (*Oxycirrhites typus*), more commonly found around the sea fans of the outer islands, such as Desroches; it is a rare visitor to Mahé. The fairy basslet (*Pseudoanthias aquamipinnis*) has got to be one of the reef's most colorful inhabitants; growing as large as 15 cm (6 in.), this active reef dweller is also well known in the Red Sea. They flit about around small recesses and along the edge of the coral reef.

Snappers such as the bluestriped snapper (*Lutjanus kasmira*) are often seen around the various wrecks in Seychelles waters; the Bengal snapper (*Lutjanus bengalensis*) is a close relation in size at 45 cm (18 in.). Oriental sweetlips (*Plectorhinchus orientalis*) are found around all of the reefs and make excellent photographic subjects, particularly the juveniles, which are very territorial and are a chocolate brown with creamy yellow vertical bands on the body. As adults, their coloration is completely different, having a yellow head and fins, black spotted, with dark grey horizontal stripes on a light blue body.

The Indian steepheaded parrotfish (*Scarus strongylocephalus*) is quite large, the supermale growing to 70 cm (28 in.). The smaller striped family groups and juveniles only grow to 10–18 cm (4–7 in.). One of the more common parrotfish to be found regularly is the bicolor parrotfish (*Cetoscarus bicolor*). Again, these fish go through several color phases before they reach the supermale size of 90 cm (3 ft).

All wrasse are born as females and move around in small social gatherings. Gradually, as they get older and reach sexual maturity, the dominant female will change sex and become male. He will then escort and protect his "harem." If he dies or is killed, the next dominant female in the hierarchy will change sex and continue the dynasty. In the wrasse family, the largest is undoubtedly the Napoleonfish (*Cheilinus undulatus*), growing to 230 cm (7 ft). It has greenish blue scrolls on its head and is blue to green overall. There are many smaller species such as the checkerboard wrasse (*Halichoeres hortulanus*) and the cleaner wrasse (*Labroides dimidiatus*), which performs the much needed service among the reef's fish communities of cleaning them of parasites and decay.

The lyretail hogfish (*Bodianus anthiodess*) and the axilspot hogfish (*Bodianus axillaris*) are both represented in the Seychelles. Gobies and blennies spend their lives living on the coral heads. They do not have swim bladders, so consequently, when they do swim, it is only in short bursts of speed.The whipcoral goby (*Bryanopsis youngei*) is one of the more comical of the species and spend their entire lives on whip corals. Steinitz's partner goby (*Amblyeleotris steinitzi*) is also well worth looking for among the coral rubble and sandy areas at the bottom of the granite boulders. They live in a burrow in association with a pistol shrimp, which excavates the burrow. They can be observed only with great care and patience.

The bigeye (*Priacanthus hamrur*) is commonly seen on night dives and is usually dark red. They drift in small groups over the edge of the deeper reefs and are active feeders in the water column at night.

The largest of the silvery predators on the reef is the great barracuda (*Sphyraena barracuda*). This fierce looking fish is usually solitary and may be found close to the mooring buoys, where it will lay in wait under the shadow of a tied-up dive boat. Barracuda can grow to 1.8 m (6 ft). Large schools of bigmouth mackerel (*Rastrelliger kanagurta*) can often be seen following the clouds of plankton in the spring and autumn.

Perhaps the fish we associate most with tropical coral reefs are the butterflyfish and angelfish. With their disc-like bodies and brilliant colors they definitely stand out in the crowd! The Koran angelfish (*Pomacanthus semicirculatus*) really is a beauty with a body decorated in shades of blue with wide concentric rings. They grow to 30 cm (12 in.) and can be fairly shy and solitary. The other more common species is the emperor angelfish (*Pomacanthus imperator*), which is dark blue underneath, ranging to yellow on top, with horizontal blue lines scales and a masked face. They are generally seen in pairs and are relatively unafraid of divers. The juveniles are completely different with a dark blue body and concentric rings starting from near the tail and spreading forward.

The regal angelfish (*Pygoplites diacanthus*) can grow to 25 cm (10 in.) and is particularly striking in color with an electric blue body running to gold tail and face with distinct vertical bands of gold, blue and black. The threespot angelfish (*Apolemichthys trimaculatus*) is a brilliant yellow with black "eyebrows" and blue lips, and is always a pleasure to find.

There are at least 14 species of butterflyfish recorded in Seychelles waters and 2 of the prettiest are Meyer's butterflyfish (*Chaetodon meyeri*) and the chevroned butterflyfish (*Chaetodon trifascialis*). Meyer's butterflyfish has a silver body with a yellow trim and black diagonal stripes through the body, face and eye. The chevroned butterflyfish, as the name indicates, has chevron markings along its body and a dark vertical band through the eye.

One of the most common species of the damselfish and chromis is the sergeant major (*Abudefduf sexfasciatus*). This is one of those species that lives in the upper water areas and is always there when food is introduced. They have five vertical black body bars and grow to 17 cm (7 in.). They can be very aggressive when protecting their eggs, as can the jewel damselfish (*Plectroglyphidodon lacrymatus*). This small oval-shaped fish has a dark body with irridescent blue spots along the back and a cream tail.

By far the most recognizable of all the fish species in the Seychelles are the clownfish or anemonefish. There are at least three recorded species in the Seychelles, including one which is indigenous to the area, the Seychelles anemonefish (*Amphiprion fuscocaudatus*), which is quite similar to Clark's anemonefish (*Amphiprion clarkii*). The third species, and incidentally most common of all of the anemonefish, is the skunk anemonefish (*Amphiprion akallopisos*), which is a creamy brown with a horizontal white line along from the tip of the nose to the tip of the tail.

Another of the fish species most associated with the Seychelles is the batfish. The longfin batfish (*Platax teira*) and the circular batfish (*Platax orbicularis*) will follow you around for most of your dive.

Always streaming past the granite outcrops and offshore coral reefs are numbers of fusiliers; one of the most common is the yellowback fusilier (*Caesio xanthonata*).

Trumpetfish are also a fairly common sight around Seychelles reefs along with their close relative the cornetfish. The trumpetfish (*Aulostomus chinensis*) can grow to 90 cm (3 ft) and have many different color variations from yellow to an almost Scottish tartan color. It is distinctive by its trumpet-shaped mouth. The coronetfish (*Fistularia commersonii*) grows up to 1.8 m (6 ft), has a long tail filament, and blue dashes or spots on the body. Shrimpfish (*Aeoliscus strigatus*) are quite rare and a delight to find as they swim around in small groups in a vertical position, with their heads pointed down.

Pufferfish and porcupinefish are quite common, as are their close relatives the boxfish. The yellowspot burrfish (*Chilomycterus spilostylus*) should not be handled, nor should any of the species, due to the possibility of their skin becoming diseased. The sharpnosed puffer (*Canthigaster valentini*) is another comical reef dweller, and they are seen regularly. The pyramid boxfish (*Tetrosomus gibbosus*) is common out on the deeper dive at Shark Bank (Dive Site No. 2), and the longnose filefish (*Oxymonacanthus longirostris*) is simply superb to watch as it explores the corals in small family groups.

Scorpionfish can be found infrequently in Seychelles waters due to their excellent camouflage techniques. They can be found more readily at night, when the divers' lights will illuminate their brightly colored pectoral fins as they move off rapidly when disturbed. The most common is the bearded scorpionfish (*Scorpaenopsis barbata*). Be careful where you put your hands, better still, stay well clear of the reef at all times. Another, sometimes maligned fish is the lionfish (*Pterois volitans*); two other species found in Seychelles waters are the spotfin lionfish (*Pterois antennata*) and clearfin lionfish (*Pterois radiata*).

Cleaning Stations. Virtually every small section of coral reef in the Seychelles Islands has cleaning stations, whether you are aware of them or not. These are areas where a number of different reef inhabitants "clean" larger fish of parasites and any diseased scales or skin.

Cleaner shrimp are very common and in fact just about all of the species of shrimp in the Seychelles act as cleaning shrimp. The largest are the peppermint shrimp (*Lysmata amboinensis*) and the coral-banded shrimp (*Stenopus hispidus*). They tend to live in and around a variety of sponges and coral caves on the granite blocks or reef wall and will signal to the waiting fish with a wave of their antennae that they are open for business. Doing a similar job on some of the larger grouper and moray eels is the hingeback cleaner shrimp (*Rhynchocinetes rugulosa*). They are known to climb into the mouths of these fish and clean any debris from the teeth.

Pacific clown anemone shrimp (*Periclimenes brevicarpalis*) live with anemones and are fairly common. This species is totally unafraid and if you extend your hand slowly, it will approach you and attempt to clean you, too! This species has been known to clean human wounds and infections successfully. To attract fish into their cleaning territory, they sway their bodies and flick their antennae similarly to the squat cleaner shrimp (*Thor amboinensis*).

Members of the wrasse family are more commonly associated with cleaning stations. Some act as roving cleaners of no fixed territory and will try their luck for a free meal of parasites from any fish that they happen to meet. The cleaning sand wrasse (*Thalassoma amblycephalum*) are specialized in cleaning very large fish and are often found in association with whale sharks. Axilspot hogfish (*Bodianus axillaris*) perform a similar function as they rove the tops of the reef crests, cleaning some of the larger reef fishes. They are much more territorial and invite larger fish to come into the cleaning station by a vertical posturing in the water column away from the reef. Jacks, normally predators, will approach the hogfish and signal their intent to be cleaned by standing on their tail, extending the jaw, and opening the mouth. The hogfish performs similarly—almost kissing—before the cleaning process can take place.

Many dramatic caves in the Seychelles outer islands provide a never-ending variety of dive adventures.

The most common of all the cleaners in the Seychelles is the common cleaner wrasse (*Labroides dimidiatus*). These small fish—up to 10 cm (3 in.)—with their black and silvery blue-striped body often work in pairs all over the hard stoney corals waiting for fish to approach their protected area of the reef. Peacock grouper (*Cephalopholus argus*) will signal its intent to be cleaned by swimming into this enclave and opening the mouth and gill covers wide. The wrasse soon enter every available space and clean off any debris, decaying skin or infection. When danger approaches, the grouper will close its mouth and gills, but still leave enough room for the wrasse to exit the much larger fish and retreat to safety before the grouper swims off. It is common to see predators and prey lining up at cleaning stations, all enmity forgotten. This social truce is integral to the survival of the fish populations on the reef. These fish are not just individuals struggling to survive, they are part of an incredibly complex integrated structure that has a firm set of guidelines that all must follow. Our short journeys into their world only allow us to see a small part of this ecosystem at work and to marvel at the complexity.

6

Safe, Smart Diving

Preparation

Before you leave home, it is essential that, if you are carrying your own personal diving equipment, it is properly serviced and in good working order. It may have been some time since your last vacation and regulators in particular are prone to "packing-up" just when you need it most. Carry an extra mask, especially if you need prescription lenses and make sure that all of your fin straps, buckles and bouyancy compensator straps are not corroded or worn. If you have done little diving, it makes excellent sense to enroll in a refresher course on arrival in the Seychelles, to reaquaint yourself, before diving on some of the deeper dive sites.

Fish Feeding

It should be pointed out that fish feeding is frowned upon by the Seychelles Department of the Environment and the Association of Professional Divers of Seychelles and the local hospitals! A number of unscrupulous dive guides still insist on feeding fish in certain areas, particularly large grouper and moray eels. This is all very well, if those divers were the only ones to visit the location (i.e., like in an aquarium). Sadly, when the next group of divers approaches this same reef, the fish automatically assume that the divers have food for them and soon start to act very aggressively when no food can be found.

All of the Seychelles dive centers and in particular the Seychelles Underwater Center have rental equipment to the highest of standards, all of which is serviced regularly, to allow you complete confidence and ease of baggage strain, particularly when traveling long distances, or combining your vacation with a stop-over in an African Game Reserve. Renting equipment that you can rely on is well worth any financial considerations.

Bouyancy Control

As an underwater photographer, I am constantly aware of the contact sometimes made with the coral reef. It is essential that all divers master the art of bouyancy control. The basic need is to be able to hover both horizontally and vertically close to the reef or the bottom without the need to touch either. Bouyancy is controlled by inflating or deflating the bouyancy compensator at various depths. Once expert bouyancy has been achieved you will notice a drastic reduction in your air consumption, you will see more marine life on each dive, and you will dramatically cut down on accidental environmental damage. Overall, your diving pleasure will increase proportionately.

For photographers, it is advised not to use extension tubes with attached framers on the lens, as this necessitates the need to touch the reef to take the photograph. Why not switch to a single lens reflex camera in a waterproof housing with the appropriate lens to allow you to take close-up photographs of the creatures without needing to touch the reef. If you must touch the reef, use only one finger for leverage to hold you still, or to push you off and then only on an area of dead coral.

Diving Accidents

Diving is a safe sport and considering the ratio of accidents to the number of divers there are, it is obvious that in most cases, training is overall to a very high standard. Accidents do happen, however, and emergency treatment should be sought immediately. The Seychelles diving operators are all equipped to handle most medical emergencies and have ship-to-shore radio to facilitate extra help, if needed. The islands' two-man recompression chamber is located in the hospital in Victoria and all of the inter-island aircraft will assist in a medical emergency.

IN AN EMERGENCY, **DIAL 999.**

Golden Rules

- Avoid touching coral with hands, fins, tanks, etc.
- Do not wear gloves.
- Never stand on coral.
- Do not collect any marine life.
- Avoid overweighting and work on bouyancy control.
- Do not feed the fish alien foods harmful to them.
- Watch your equipment consoles; do not drag on the coral.
- Do not use spear guns.
- Do not molest marine life, in particular turtles, pufferfish, and sea urchins.
- Do not climb inside barrel sponges.

Hazardous Marine Life

Anemones, corals, and jellyfish are armed with a battery of stinging cells called "nematocists." These cells are actually a tiny barbed harpoon tipped with a paralyzing poison that the creature will fire into its prey should they happen to brush against them. These microscopic cells are particularly affective in the case of the Portugese man-of-war, whose tentacles can trail underneath more than 10 m (33 ft). Local remedies are known for these stings.

For many first-time divers and snorkelers, their introduction to fire coral (*Millepora alcicornis*) can be a painful and unforgettable experience. Fire coral is not actually a true coral but a member of the hydroid family or sea fern. They have a hard calcerous skeleton either branching or in bony plates. The "coral" is covered in thousands of tiny barbed hooks which can penetrate the skin and leave large irritations that easily last for several days. They can be found in most areas of the reef and will often completely smother the larger granite rock outcrops found on Brissaire Rocks and Trois Bancs (Dive Site Nos. 2 & 18).

A stonefish envenomation can be lethal, but what the local Seychellois call stonefish are actually a species of scorpionfish, which are not as harmful. The humpback scorpionfish (*Scorpaenopsis gibbosa*) is common around all of the Seychelles reefs and although it looks "nasty," it is only very rarely fatal.

Some molluscs also have a nasty surprise for those who like to collect shells. Cone shells in particular have a very sharp spike that can be fired from their "foot" to paralyze their prey; this can penetrate the skin. A wound from the geography cone shell (*Conus geographus*) can be fatal. If in doubt, DO NOT TOUCH.

Wounds from sea urchin spines usually occur when diving where there is oceanic swell or surge. The movement of the sea can push you into these long-spined sea urchins (*Diadema setosum*), whose spines are very fragile and can snap off easily once in the skin. Great care should be taken when diving or snorkeling in such conditions.

Stingrays can inflict a nasty wound from their tail if you step on them accidentally, but generally, they are much too timid and will never attack divers willingly.

Moray eels do not pose a threat, unless you put your hand down carelessly on the coral in front of them, or try to handle or feed them. The rule in the Seychelles is " Keep your hands and your equipment off the coral at all times and do not feed the fish."

Conservation

Project Aware. Ten ways a diver can protect the Aquatic Realm (Produced by PADI):

- Dive carefully in fragile aquatic ecosystems, such as coral reefs.
- Be aware of your body and equipment placement when diving.

- Keep your diving skills sharp with continuing education.
- Consider your impact on aquatic life through your interactions.
- Understand and respect underwater life.
- Resist the urge to collect souvenirs.
- If you hunt and/or gather game, obey all fish and game laws.
- Report environmental disturbances or destruction of your dive sites.
- Be a role model for other divers in diving and non-diving interaction with the environment.
- Get involved in local environmental activities and issues.

Marine Reserves. The island of Praslin has one marine reserve—Curieuse Marine National Park. It covers all of the area around the headlands that flank Curieuse Bay to the northeast of Praslin out and around Curieuse Island, where most of the recreational diving takes place. Praslin is also home to the Vallée de Mai National Park, located in the southern central region of the island on the main road between Baie Ste Anne and Grand' Anse. The Vallée de Mai has been declared a World Heritage Site by UNESCO.

There are three national marine nature reserves on the main island of Mahé. St. Anne National Marine Nature Reserve due east of Victoria encompasses Aaint Anne Island, Moyenne Island, Long Island, Cerf Island, and their smaller islets. This is an extremely popular area with daily visits by glass-bottom boat. The shallow lagoon between the islands is particularly lovely. Diving is done on the outer edges of the marine park around the Beacon Rock area only during the winter months, when the prevailing westerly winds make the conditions too difficult for launching dive boats from Beau Vallon Bay.

Baie Ternay Marine National Park is located in the sheltered area of the northwestern side of Mahé on the way west to Conception Island. It encompasses all of the seaward area of the bay including the fringing coral reef out to Matoopa Point. Port Launay Marine National Park is on the other side of Cape Matoopa to the southwest. Both marine parks are a natural extension to the Morne Seychellois National Park, which encompasses much of the terrestrial vegetation from Victoria in the east to Bel Ombre in the north and Grand' Anse in the west. Both marine reserves can be reached by road from Port Glaud. Port Launay and Baie Ternay are very popular with snorkelers, with Baie Ternay being the best choice for divers, who always approach by boat.

Appendix: Dive Operators and Services

Mahé

The Association of Professional Divers of Seychelles (APDS)
PO Box 167
Victoria, Mahé
Seychelles
Tel/Fax: (248) 344223

Deep Thoughts Reef Diving Center
Le Meridien Barbarons
PO Box 540
Victoria, Mahé
Tel: (248) 378253; Fax: (248) 378484

Diables des Mers Diving Centre
PO Box 477
Beau Vallon Beach, Mahé
Tel: (248) 247104; Fax: (248) 241776

Jules Verne (Pty) Ltd.
Anse Aux Poules Bleues
Mahé
Tel: (248) 361450

Marine Divers International
Berjaya Beau Vallon Beach Resort
Mahé
Tel: (248) 247141; Fax: (248) 247809

Pro-Diving (Sey) Ltd.
Plantation Club Hotel
Mahé
Tel: (248) 376158; Fax: (248) 361333

Rainbow Divers
Northolme Hotel
Glacis, Mahé
Tel: (248) 261222; Fax: (248) 2261223

Speedy Aquatics Dive Center
Berjaya Mahe Beach Hotel
PO Box 540
Victoria, Mahé
Tel: (248) 378451; Fax: (248) 378517

Sheraton Dive Center
PO Box 540
Port Glaud, Mahé
Tel: (248) 378451; Fax: (248) 378517

Underwater Center Seychelles
PO Box 384
Coral Strand Hotel
Beau Vallon Beach, Mahé
Tel: (248) 247357; Fax: (248) 344223

Praslin

Michel Gardette, Aqua Diving,
Anse Volbert, Praslin
Tel: (248) 233972; Fax: (248) 233340

Praslin Beach Watersports
Berjaya Praslin Beach
Anse Volbert, Praslin
Tel: (248) 232019; Fax: (248) 232148

Underwater Center Praslin
Paradise Sun Hotel, Anse Volbert,
Praslin
Tel: (248) 232222;
(248) Fax: 232148

La Digue

La Digue Lodge Dive Center,
La Digue
Tel: (248) 234232; Fax: (248) 234366

Silhouette

Silhouette Lodge Dive Center
PO Box 608
Silhouette
Tel: (248) 224003; Fax: (248) 224897

Miscellaneous Travel Services

Aqua Diving Services Pty Ltd
PO Box 601
Praslin
Tel: (248) 233972;
Fax: (248) 233015

Fantasea Cruises
PO Box 234 Hofit, 40295
Israel
Tel: (248)(972) (053) 666482;
Fax: (053) 663262

Brownie Marine Services
PO Box 470
Victoria, Mahé.
Tel: (248) 378627

Yacht Connections
c/o Anne Casebourne,
The Hames, Church Road
South Ascot, Berkshire,
England SL5 9DP
Tel: +44 (01344) 24987;
Fax: +44 (01344) 26849

Seychelles Tourist Offices

Belgium, Netherlands, and Luxemburg
157 Boulevard du Jubilee
Bruxelles
Tel: (32 2) 4255989;
Fax: (32 2) 4260629

France and Switzerland
(French Speaking)
32 Rue de Ponthieu
75008 Paris
Tel: (33 1) 42899777;
Fax: (33 1) 4289770

Germany, Austria and Switzerland
(German Speaking)
Hoch Strasse 15
D-6000 Frankfurt Am Main
Tel: (49 69) 292064/5;
Fax: (49 69) 296230

Italy
Via Guilia 66
00186 Rome
Tel: (395) 6869056;
Fax: (396) 6868127

Japan
Berna Heits 4 - A3
Hiroo 5-4-11
Shibuya, Tokyo 150
Tel: (81 3) 54490461;
Fax: (81 3) 54490462

Kenya and South Africa
Jubilee Insurance, Exchange Building,
3rd Floor
Box 30702
Nairobi
Tel: (254 2) 221335;
Fax: (254 2) 219787

Reunion
4 residence Pointe des Jardins
1, Rue Juliette Dodue
97400 St. Denis
Tel: (262) 418788; Fax: (262) 212600

Seychelles Department of Tourism and Transport
Independence House
PO Box 92
Victoria, Mahé
Republic of Seychelles
Tel: (248) 25313; Fax: (248) 24035

Spain and Portugal
Zurbano 26 Bis, 1° Pta
28010 Madrid, Spain
Tel: (0341) 3192341;
Fax: (0341) 3198359

United States of America and Canada
820 2nd Avenue
Suite 900F 3927 F
New York 10017-4504
Tel: (212) 6879766;
Fax: (212) 9229177

United Kingdom, Eire, and Scandanavia
2nd Floor, Eros House
111 Baker Street
London W1M 1FE
Tel: (44 171) 2241670;
Fax: (44 171) 4861352

Seychelles Tourism Representatives

Singapore
Siam Express (Pte) Ltd.
15 Beach Road
#05-10 Beach Center
Singapore 189677
Tel: (65) 3399727; Fax: (65) 3393220

India
TRAC Representations (India) Pvt Ltd.
F-12 Connaught Place
New Delhi 110001
Tel: (91 1) 1331122; Fax: (91 1) 13350270

Israel
Open Sky Ltd.
El Al Building, 32 Ben Yehuda Street
Tel Aviv 63805
Tel: (972) 35253444; Fax: (972) 35253445

Air Seychelles Offices

Air Seychelles has representatives throughout the world. Addresses, telephone and fax numbers for specific countries are available from Air Seychelles Head Office:

Air Seychelles
Victoria House
PO Box 386
Victoria, Mahé
Seychelles
Tel: (248) 318000; Fax: (248) 225159

United Kingdom
Aviareps
Premier House, Betts Way
Crawley, West Sussex
Tel: (+44) (01293) 529429;
Fax: (+44) (01293) 51229

United States of America
APS Inc., N. America
5757 W Century Boulevard, Suite 660
Los Angeles, California 90045
Tel: (1-310) 3767465;
Fax: (1-310) 3380708

Bibliography

Seychelles (Political Castaways), Christopher Lee, Elm Tree Books, London, 1976

Journey Through Seychelles, Mahamed Amin & Ducan Willetts, Camerapix Publishers, Nairobi, 1994

Indian Ocean Tropical Fish Guide, Helmut Debelius, Aquaprint, Germany, 1993

Seychelles In Your Pocket, Leon Viola Explorer, Seychelles, 1993/95

Reef Fishes of the Indian Ocean, Dr. Gerald Allen & Roger Steene, TFH Publications, New Jersey, USA, 1987

Indo-Pacific Coral Reef Guide, Dr. Gerald Allen & Roger Steene, Tropical Reef Research, Singapore, 1994

The Marine Atlas, Helmut Debelius & Hans Baensch, Tetra Press, Germany, 1994

Tropical Pacific Invertibrates, Patrick Colin & Charles Arneson, Coral Reef Press Publications, California, USA, 1995

Seychelles, Peter Vine, Immel, U.K., 1989

The Seychelles, G. Lionnet, David & Charles, U.K., 1972

Fishes of Seychelles, JLB & MM Smith, JLB Smith Institute of Icthyology, South Africa, 1969

Index

 **Pisces Books®**

Be sure to check out these other great books from Pisces:

Caribbean Reef Ecology
Great Reefs of the World
Skin Diver Magazine's Book of Fishes, 2nd Edition
Shooting Underwater Video: A Complete Guide to the Equipment and Techniques for
    Shooting, Editing, and Post-Production
Snorkeling . . . Here's How
Watching Fishes: Understanding Coral Reef Fish Behavior
Watersports Guide to Cancun

Diving and Snorkeling Guides to:

Australia: Coral Sea and Great Barrier Reef
Australia: Southeast Coast and Tasmania
The Bahamas: Family Islands and Grand
    Bahama
The Bahamas: Nassau and New Providence
    Island, 2nd Ed.
Bali
Belize
The Best Caribbean Diving
Bonaire
The British Virgin Islands
California's Central Coast
The Cayman Islands, 2nd Ed.
Cozumel, 2nd Ed.
Cuba
Curacao
Fiji
Florida's East Coast, 2nd Ed.
The Florida Keys, 2nd Ed.

The Great Lakes
Guam and Yap
The Hawaiian Islands, 2nd Ed.
Jamaica
Northern California and the Monterey
    Peninsula, 2nd Ed.
The Pacific Northwest
Palau
Puerto Rico
The Red Sea
Roatan and Honduras' Bay Islands, 2nd Ed.
Scotland
St. Maarten, Saba, and St. Eustatius
Southern California, 2nd Ed.
Texas, 2nd Ed.
Truk Lagoon
The Turks and Caicos Islands
The U.S. Virgin Islands, 2nd Ed.
Vanuatu

Available from your favorite dive shop, bookstore, or directly from the publisher: Pisces Books®, a division of Gulf Publishing company, Book Division, Dept. AD, P.O. Box 2608, Houston, Texas 77252-2608. (713) 520-4444.

Include purchase price plus $4.95 for shipping and handling. IL, NJ, PA, and TX residents add appropriate tax.